When You Lie Down & When You Rise Up

Daily Readings in Vayikra - Leviticus

Rabbi Jonathan Allen

Preface by Rabbi Carl Kinbar

When You Lie Down & When You Rise Up
Daily Readings in Vayikra - Leviticus
ISBN 1-901917-11-8
Copyright © 2011 Jonathan Peter Allen

Cover Design by Naomi Allen

Typeset in Times New Roman, Viner Hand, Aquaduct, Briner Pro

Published by Elisheva Publishing Ltd.
www.elishavepublishing.co.uk

Contents

Preface

I have known Jonathan Allen for many years and he has always impressed me as a godly and serious man of God as well as a diligent student of the Word. In these studies in the book of Vayikra/Leviticus, he brings his characteristic thoroughness and spirituality to bear on the words of *Torah*, weaving in insights by some of the foremost commentators in Jewish history, such as the classical commentators Rashi (Rabbi Shlomo ben Yitzhaki) and Ramban (Nachmanides) as well as modern commentators such as Samson Raphael Hirsch and Nechama Leibowitz. He is also alert to the crucial function of the *B'rit Hadasha* to draw out implications of the *Torah* for today.

While these studies are educational in nature, providing us with insights into the *Torah* and Jewish tradition, they have a strong spiritual focus on relationship with God. They embody a pietistic approach to spiritual life, with its characteristic sensitivity to sin as the most problematic element of life. Here he draws on traditional Jewish sources and *B'rit Hadashah* readings that exemplify this approach.

A sample of Jonathan's commentary can be found in the study on Vayikra 4:2 ("If a soul sins in a sin of ignorance from all the commandments of Adonai that should not be done ..."). He observes that "Nachmanides is concerned about the effects of even unintentional sin in our lives: 'All sins (even if committed unwittingly) produce a particular "stain" upon the soul and constitute a blemish thereon, and the soul is only worthy to be received by the countenance of its Creator when it is pure of all sin. Were it not so, then all the fools of the world would be deserving to come before Him.' He seems to be saying that the smallest infraction, even on a completely ignorant basis or committed by someone who is incapable of understanding or remembering the commandments, is still sin and so requires atonement." In the same study, Jonathan brings in the *B'rit Hadashah*: "The all-encompassing nature of sin is clearly picked up by James when he wrote to the Jewish people in the *Diaspora* who had come to faith in Yeshua as the Messiah of Israel: 'For a person who keeps the whole Torah, yet stumbles at one point, has become guilty of breaking them all' (James 2:10, CJB)."

Mr. Allen does not construe these as abstract principles but seeks to aid the reader in applying them today. Therefore, he concludes the chapter, as he does each of these studies, with a section of application to our lives today.

For the reader who is inexperienced in Jewish sources or in applying the *B'rit Hadashah* in its naturally Jewish way, I recommend these studies as fine introductory studies that do not overwhelm with an overabundance of information but maintains a steady focus on core issues of the *Torah*. From my perspective, it is particularly important that they represent not only Mr. Allen's perspectives on the *Torah* and spiritual matters but his heart and life as I have known them these many years.

Rabbi Carl Kinbar

Introduction

This third book of the Bible - Leviticus - is the point at which many people who have set out to read the Bible from cover to cover, give up. Over time it has come to be seen as a book that is irrelevant in both the Jewish and Christians worlds: the Jewish world because there is no Temple and after 2000 years, many Jews are not necessarily enthusiastic about restarting blood sacrifices; the replacement-driven Christian world because the Mosaic Law has all been done away with by the sacrifice of Yeshua. Nevertheless, on closer examination and with a little help from the ancient commentators, we find that these texts still have a lot to teach us about holiness, purity and other qualities to which the believer in Yeshua - and therefore, a follower of the God of Israel - is still expected to aspire.

In preparing these commentaries for publication one after another in one book rather than reading them a year apart as they were originally written, we became aware that some of the texts seem very similar. However, the commentaries do all have their own distinctive theme and message, so please bear with us as you read and together we tease out the subtleties and meanings that are there in the original.

These texts describe in great detail much of the cultic ritual concerning the various classes of sacrificial offering - burnt, guilt, sin, freewill and peace - and the circumstances that govern their usage and practice. The High Priest's inauguration and the ritual for *Yom Kippur* is then related, together with an extensive set of rules, known as the Holiness Code, concerning co-sanguinous relationships, authorised food and the festival calendar. Finally, the book covers infectious diseases in both people, clothing and houses while dealing with various kinds of bodily functions and impurities. Hardly applicable, many would say, to our modern world, yet in the typical Jewish way, worthy of study. How would we know what the commandment to "Be holy!" meant if the text did not tell us?

These commentaries on the weekly *Torah* portion have been written over the course of seven years: one per portion, per year. They have grown as we have grown; they have developed as our knowledge and understanding of the Hebrew texts, the classic and modern commentators has also developed. Like us, they are themselves a work-in-progress. They step in turn through the seven readings or *aliyot* into which the weekly portion is divided, to offer seven commentaries in each portion. You can read one at a time for each day of the week, or dip into them on an *ad hoc* basis.

This work is, in a sense, "old hat" in that they have been published week by week on our website: *http://www.messianictrust.org.uk* and, indeed, new commentaries continue to be published each week. Please do visit the website or sign up for the weekly e-mail to join in the ongoing conversation and have your say on the thoughts presented.

We have resisted the temptation to rewrite or enlarge the earlier commentaries, believing that their value lies in what - we trust - God has been saying, rather than in the cleverness (or otherwise) of the words or the number of citations. We have nevertheless taken the opportunity to remove some spelling mistakes and typographical issues, hopefully without inserting a fresh collection during the collation and editing phase.

It is true to say that the body of Messiah outside the Messianic Jewish world has largely ignored and rejected the work of the Jewish rabbis in discussing and processing - often at great length - the words of *Torah*, God's foundational revelation to the patriarchs and the people of Israel. This has been a significant loss to the body, as many early insights into the multiple layers of meaning and nuance within the text have essentially been denied to the believing community. One of the aims of these commentaries has been to share some of the insights, commonly held among Jewish people from Second Temple times - the times of Yeshua's (Jesus') own earthly ministry - and successive generations, with the wider body of Messiah. In particular, it is our desire and - we believe - calling, to encourage our own people to re-discover the riches of the rabbinic writings and hear the ancient voices and conversations afresh in the light of our faith in Yeshua, the Jewish Messiah.

Technicalities

We usually follow the Ashkenazic division of the *parasha* into the seven readings in which the text is read during the *Torah* service on *Shabbat*.

As this is a work based upon the Hebrew Bible, we have followed a number of conventions of the Jewish world that may need some explanation:

a. names: we use Hebrew names for Yeshua (Jesus), Rav Sha'ul (the Apostle Paul), the patriarchs, Moshe and Aharon, the books of the *Torah* and the individual *parasha* names; this is of no doctrinal significance, but is part of our culture as Messianic Jews

Avraham	Abraham	B'resheet	Genesis
Yitz'khak	Isaac	Shemot	Exodus
Ya'akov	Jacob	Vayikra	Leviticus
Moshe	Moses	B'Midbar	Numbers
Aharon	Aaron	D'varim	Deuteronomy

b. the chapter and verse numbering of the traditional Hebrew text: this is occasionally different from the conventional English numbering and most often only varies by one or two verses; we usually follow the numbering of the Bible version from which we are quoting

There is one commentary for each of the seven *aliyot*; seven commentaries in each portion. These can be read one at a time for each day of the week, or dipped into on an *ad hoc* basis. Each commentary contains a short Hebrew text, its transliteration into an English character set and an English translation, followed by a commentary based upon the text, some verses or passages for further study and some application suggestions.

Leap years - the Jewish calendar has seven leap years in each nineteen year cycle, when we add an extra month to the year - often a challenge to the *parasha* sequence. In non-leap years, some of the portions are traditionally read together; in leap years, they are read separately. The reader will find that while the double portions have full coverage, the single portions do not have a full complement of seven commentaries each.

Citations from the ancient Jewish writings - the Mishnah, the Talmuds and the Midrash Rabbah are accompanied by their appropriate references. The prefix "*m.*" means Mishnah, "*y.*" the Jerusalem Talmud, "*b.*" the

Babylonian Talmud. Each part of Midrash Rabbah is given its Hebrew name, for example Vayikra Rabbah. Talmud references give the page (or folio) number in normal type, while the side *a* or *b* in italic.

References to the classic commentators show their names in the Aquaduct font; there are brief biographical details listed for each named source in the Biography section at the end of the book. These are intended to provide a frame or context from which the commentator speaks. Author and book names also share the Aquaduct font and can be found in the Bibliography section, at the end of the book.

Terms and expressions in an italic typeface are explained in the Glossary section at the end of the book. This provides definitions of some of the other documents, languages and factual information that are referenced in the commentaries, or explain some of the terms that may be unfamiliar to modern readers or those from a less Jewish-friendly background.

Quotations from the Scriptures themselves are shown in Brinar Pro font so that they are distinct from the commentary text.

One particular Jewish convention is used with such frequency that although it has glossary entries, we felt that we should explain it here as well. It is Jewish custom not to use or pronounce the tetragrammaton covenant name of God in an inappropriate or irreverent way in order to fulfill the commandment not to take God's name in vain. Jewish custom is therefore to use one of two allusions to allow the name of God to be used and referred to in a "safe" way. Obviously, the tetragrammaton appears many times in the Hebrew biblical text. When formally read or used in a worship context, the word is pronounced *Adonai*; on other occasions it is pronounced *HaShem*, which literally means "The Name". You will find these words used in many places in the commentaries.

Every book that includes transliteration of Hebrew words into an English alphabet has its own particular style. The purpose of the transliteration is to provide a pronunciation that also reflects the different letters where possible. We denote the Hebrew letter *chaf* by 'ch', *khet* by 'kh' and *kof* by 'k'. A *chaf* with a *dagesh* (a dot in the middle of the letter) is also shown as 'k'. We represent both *sin* and *samech* by 's' and *tzadi* by 'tz'. Dipthongs are usually shown by adding an 'i' or 'y' to the ordinary vowel letter. We generally follow modern Israeli pronunciation, so *vav* has a 'v' sound and *tav* and *tet* are both always 't'. In particular we do not follow the Ashkenazic custom of pronouncing a *tav* without a dagesh as 's'.

We do not take account in this book of *Rosh Chodesh* or the "special" *shabbaton* during the year, such as *Shabbat Shekalim* or *Shabbat Shuva*, when some of the ordinary readings may be replaced by an otherwise out-of-sequence reading. Readings for the festivals will be found at the end of the normal weekly readings, before the reference sections.

וַיִּקְרָא

Vayikra - And He called

Vayikra / Leviticus 1:1 - 6:8

רִאשׁוֹן	Aliyah One	Vayikra/Leviticus 1:1 - 13
שֵׁנִי	Aliyah Two	Vayikra/Leviticus 1:14 - 2:6
שְׁלִישִׁי	Aliyah Three	Vayikra/Leviticus 2:7 - 16
רְבִיעִי	Aliyah Four	Vayikra/Leviticus 3:1 - 17
חֲמִשִׁי	Aliyah Five	Vayikra/Leviticus 4:1 - 26
שִׁשִּׁי	Aliyah Six	Vayikra/Leviticus 4:27 - 5:10
שְׁבִיעִי	Aliyah Seven	Vayikra/Leviticus 5:11 - 26

וַיִּקְרָא א׳

Vayikra - And He called - 1

Vayikra / Leviticus 1:1 - 13

Vayikra/Leviticus 1:1 He called to Moshe, and Adonai spoke to him from the Tent of Meeting

וַיִּקְרָא אֶל-מֹשֶׁה וַיְדַבֵּר יהוה אֵלָיו מֵאֹהֶל
mey'ohel eylayv Adonai vay'dabeyr Moshe el vayikra

מוֹעֵד
mo'ed

Why does the *Torah* tell us that God called Moshe and then spoke to him? Rashi points out that calling and speaking are not the same: one is for getting someone's attention and the other is for communication. In his vision of the Lord, Isaiah saw the heavenly beings in the presence of God, that "one called out to another and said, 'Holy ...'" (Isaiah 6:3, NASB). Rashi suggests that calling Moshe by name was a sign of God's favour and intimacy with Moshe, for when God speaks Balaam the Hebrew text uses a very similar word, וַיִּקָּר, (*vayikar*), which is translated "God met Balaam" (B'Midbar 23:4, NASB). God is intimate with those He loves and distant with those who are evil.

Throughout history God has been calling people to turn to Him in repentance so that He may enter into relationship with them and forgive their sins. "'Come now, and let us reason together,' says the Lord, 'though your sins are as scarlet, they will be white as snow'" (Isaiah 1:18, NASB). From the time that God first called out to Adam in the garden, "Adonai, God, called to the man, 'Where are you?'" (B'resheet 3:9, CJB), God has been seeking and searching for men and women who will respond to His call so that He may speak to them and show them His ways.

When Yeshua started His ministry, He called a group of disciples together. "As Yeshua walked by Lake Kinneret, He saw two brothers ... Yeshua said them, 'Come after Me, and I will make you fishers for men!' At once they left their nets and went with Him. Going on from there, He saw two other brothers ... and He called them. At once they left the boat and their father and went with

Yeshua" (Matthew 4:18-22, CJB). Yeshua called and the disciples responded - they went with Him - so that He could teach them about the Kingdom of God. Before they could hear His words about the kingdom, they had to be in relationship with Him.

Further Study: Matthew 3:1-6; Matthew 4:12-17

Application: How is God speaking to you today? Are you in intimate conversation with Him or do you hear Him calling from afar? Use today to draw near to God and respond to His call that He may build a relationship with you.

וַיִּקְרָא ב׳

Vayikra - And He called - 2

Vayikra / Leviticus 1:14 - 2:6

Vayikra/Leviticus 1:14 ... he shall bring from the turtle-doves or from the young doves his offering

וְהִקְרִיב מִן־הַתֹּרִים אוֹ מִן־בְּנֵי הַיּוֹנָה

hayonah b'ney min o hatoriym min v'hikriyv

אֶת־קָרְבָּנוֹ:

korbano et

The first chapter of Vayikra deals with the burnt offering, that which goes up entirely in smoke to the Lord, with neither the offerer or the priest having any benefit from its meat. Although the earlier verses talk of offerings from the flock or herd, this verse says that the offering may also be from the doves or pigeons. Rashi suggests that in fact the offering could be as small as one single turtle-dove or young pigeon. Abravanel makes the comment to the start of the instructions in verse 2 that the Hebrew word order doesn't say "if any man of you bring an offering" but "if any man bring of you an offering", so that the text can be understood as saying that the offering is a sacrifice of oneself. He goes on, "if he brings it willingly before the Lord - if he submits all his being and will before the Lord. It thus speaks of the obligations to present oneself with all one's power and mental force, intellect and desires to serve God and cleave to Him." Hence this text: the size or the species is not important; anything that is accessible is allowed (Ramban) because it is the heart attitude of the giver in which God is most interested.

Some centuries later, God speaks to the people involved with the service in the first Temple: "I'm fed up with burnt offerings and rams and the fat of fattened animals! I get no pleasure from the blood of bulls, lambs and goats!" (Isaiah 1:11, CJB). Weren't these the regular morning and evening sacrifices that the Lord had commanded through Moshe, the burnt sacrifices to be a pleasing aroma before Him? Why is God now rejecting them? The answer comes just a few verses later: "When you spread out your hands, I will hide My eyes from you; no matter how much you pray, I won't be listening; because your hands are covered with blood" (Isaiah 1:15, CJB). God made it very clear that the offerings were unacceptable because the hearts of the people were wrong; the offerings were the result of oppression and injustice.

One day Yeshua was in the (second) Temple with His *talmidim* and they saw many people pouring money into the offering boxes - not an unusual sight or sound. But Yeshua "noticed a poor widow drop in two small coins. He said, 'I can guarantee this truth: this poor widow has given more than all the others. All of these people have given what they could spare. But she, in her poverty, has given everything she had to live on'" (Luke 21:2-3, GWT). The Master didn't say that any of the other, larger offerings were insufficient or inadequate in any way, He simply compared the givers: those who given much had done so from their plenty; the offering may have been exactly the 'right' amount or even more, but it was given from a position of wealth. Although the widow's offering was much smaller, it was just as acceptable and of greater value than the others because of her poverty and her heart towards God.

Further Study: 2 Corinthians 9:6-13

Application: Do we wince when an offering is taken up or are we glad to contribute to God's work, even if we can give but a small amount compared to other people? God is more interested in us than our money and when we give ourselves that is more valuable to Him than the largest amounts of money.

וַיִּקְרָא ג׳

Vayikra - And He called - 3

Vayikra / Leviticus 2:7 - 16

Vayikra/Leviticus 2:7 And if your offering is a grain-offering in a deep vessel

וְאִם־מִנְחַת מַרְחֶשֶׁת קָרְבָּנֶךָ

kar'banecha mar'kheshet min'kha v'im

מִנְחָה, here ending with a **ת** *tav* rather than a **ה** *hay,* because it is in construct form, means literally 'gift' but is used to refer to grain, flour or meal offerings. As well as being a required part of many of the animal offerings - which are to be accompanied by both grain and wine offerings - a grain offering may be free-standing offering in its own right. Only the memorial potion is actually offered on the altar; the bulk of the offering is given to the priests to eat.

Hirsch suggests that the grain offering expresses our acknowledgement to *HaShem* in respect of "our food, comfort and satisfaction - our happiness in life" and points out that the many different ways the grain offering can be made reflects the many ways in which God blesses us, not just in necessity but also in the extras that we could do without. So God loves a deep-pan offering as much as we do!

Nachmanides (the Ramban) comments for all the classes of grain offering that while it is the priest that actually offers the מִנְחָה before the Lord, it is the individual that is making the offering who mixes mixes the oil and the flour and, if it is a cooked grain offering, cooks it before bringing it to the *cohen*. This is an important level of involvement and participation for every person who makes this offering; not only do they provide the material, but unlike the animal offerings where the priest does all the preparation, each individual prepares the offering with their own hands.

Nechama Leibowitz points out that the early Sages emphasised that a poor man's meal offering - instead of the more costly, but for him, out of reach, burnt offering - was considered superior: as if he had offered up himself. "A woman once brought a handful of flour, whereupon the priest scorned her, saying 'See what these offer us! It will do neither for a meal nor for the altar!' This *cohen* was addressed in a dream: Do not scorn her, it is as if she had offered up her very soul" (Vayikra Rabbah 3:5). The Talmud puts these words in God's mouth: "Whose habit is it to bring a meal offering? It is the poor man's. I consider it as if he had offered his very soul to Me" (*b*. Menakhot 104*b*).

We know that Yeshua took the opportunity to emphasise this principle in monetary terms when He was in the Temple with His *talmidim* (Luke 21:1-4, CJB), but there is more to it than that. The Scriptures had already said of Him that "a bruised reed he will not break, and a faintly burning wick he will not quench" (Isaiah 42:3, ESV) and that "He will tend his flock like a shepherd; he will gather the lambs in his arms; he will carry them in his bosom, and gently lead those that are with young" (Isaiah 40:11, ESV). He is interested in the smallest of things from the least of people and considers them equal to the largest things from what the world sees as the most important people - they are all the same in God's economy and precious in His sight.

Further Study: D'varim 16:16-17; Acts 2:44-45; Revelation 8:2-4

Application: No matter how small and insignificant you may feel, God values everything that you are. He isn't after your money, He wants you! Whether rich or poor, the variety and joy of a life offered to Him is always pleasing in His sight.

וַיִּקְרָ֖א 'ד

Vayikra - And He called - 4

Vayikra / Leviticus 3:1 - 17

Vayikra/Leviticus 3:1 And if his offering is a sacrifice of peace-offerings ...

... וְאִם־זֶבַח שְׁלָמִים

sh'lamiym zevakh v'im

The word שְׁלָמִים has attracted attention from many commentators. A noun derived from the root שָׁלַם, to be whole or complete, its usual translation of "peace-offerings" is more a reflection of the Vulgate Latin translation *pacificus*, while the Septuagint gives it no less than three different translations. Levine points out that there is now evidence that the term originally meant "tribute, gift of greeting"; in *Akkadian* and *Ugaritic* texts the cognate[1] terms are used to describe the gifts presented by vassals to their suzerains[2] when they visited them, or by ambassadors when on a diplomatic mission to allies. In this sense, it is much more difficult to sit and eat with people with whom you are in violent disagreement unless there has been some form of reconciliation. So within the Temple system, the peace offering expressed a peaceful relationship between God and the people, reaffirmed by the sacrifice itself.

Rashi makes two comments: first that they bring peace into the world - because they are offered as a means of showing or making peace - and secondly "because there is peace in them, for the altar, for the priest and for the owner." All who are involved in the process receive a portion of the offering: part is burnt on the altar as the Lord's portion, the breast and part of the right hind leg go to the *cohanim* and the rest goes to those who bring the offering and it is to be eaten that day. All are seen to be participating in the peace-offering: God Himself, the priest as God's representative, and the people who brought the offering; not only do they participate in the process

---

1. cognates are words - in one or more languages - that have a common origin, meaning that they are descended from the same word, possibly in a common predecessor language.
2. a suzerain is an over-king; a powerful king to whom other (lesser, smaller) kings are vassals or tributary while retaining some limited autonomy.

and the meat, but they are also seen as participating in the peace, the fellowship of taking part in a shared meal.

In His early teaching in the Galil, Yeshua taught: "Blessed are the peacemakers, for they shall be called the sons of God" (Matthew 5:9, NASB). One of the ways that Jewish tradition portrays Aharon, the High Priest, is in the role of peace maker - that he would go around the camp making peace between those in conflict, resolving arguments and negotiating disputes to bring about peaceful resolution. Anyone who has spent time working in the counselling, political or arbitration arenas - be that industrial relations, marriage counselling, international treaties or sibling rivalry - knows that it can be very hard work to make peace. Note that there is a big difference between a peacemaker and a peacekeeper; while the latter will attempt to smooth over differences and keep things ticking over without erupting into conflict, it is only the peacemaker who will force the differences and disagreements out into the open so that they can be resolved, even if that does mean a short-term increase in hostilities. Yeshua didn't call us to be peacekeepers, although we often seem to be engaged in that activity, but to be peacemakers: engaging with people and situations to resolve conflicts rather than hiding them or pretending that they don't exist.

That, after all, is the example He set us on the cross by providing the only possible solution to our broken relationships with God. Rav Sha'ul wrote: "We have peace with God through Yeshua the Messiah" (Romans 5:1). What did he mean by that? He goes on to explain: "while we were yet sinners, Messiah died for us" (v. 8); "while we were enemies, we were reconciled to God through the death of His Son" (v. 10). Writing to those at Colossi, Sha'ul added, "through Him, [God] reconciled all things to Himself, having made peace through the blood of His cross" (Colossians 1:20, NASB). Knowing that the issue of sin could not be swept under the carpet or simply ignored, Yeshua was not only our sin-offering, offering His body as a sacrifice to take away sin, and our Passover Lamb, so that His blood causes the destroyer to pass over us, but He is also our peace offering - He made peace between us and God so that relationship might be restored. The shared meal of the peace offering becomes ours as Yeshua said: "Here, I'm standing at the door, knocking. If someone hears My voice and opens the door, I will come into him and eat with him, and he will eat with Me" (Revelation 3:20, CJB).

Further Study: Judges 6:17-24; Proverbs 16:7; Hebrews 12:14

Application: Have you really made peace with God, or have you accepted His forgiveness in Yeshua while carefully keeping your distance in case He turns round and zaps you? Today would be a fine day to sit down and chew over the peace offering that Yeshua made for us and really get to know Him close up, for He is our peace.

וַיִּקְרָא 'ה

Vayikra - And He called - 5

Vayikra / Leviticus 4:1 - 26

Vayikra/Leviticus 4:2 If a soul sins in a sin of ignorance from all the commandments of Adonai that should not be done ...

נֶפֶשׁ כִּי־תֶחֱטָא בִשְׁגָגָה מִכֹּל מִצְוֹת יהוה
Adonai mitzvot mikol bishgaga tekheta kiy nephesh

אֲשֶׁר לֹא תֵעָשֶׂינָה
tey'aseynah lo asher

Nechama Leibowitz says that, "sin offerings are brought only for transgressions committed unwittingly" and goes on to ask the question: "Why is an error, the result of inattention, considered a sin?" Torat Kohanim connects this to the verse, "You shall have one law for him who does anything unintentionally, for him who is a native among the sons of Israel and for the alien who sojourns among them" (B'Midbar 15:29, NASB), to explain that the sin offering for unintentional idolatry is the model for all unintentional sin offerings: in all cases where a negative command or prohibition ("You shall not ...") is violated unintentionally, a sin offering must be brought to atone for the violation.

There are three Hebrew verbs that sound very similar: שָׁגַג, the root that generates the noun בִשְׁגָגָה - in a sin of ignorance - in our text, means "to err, to commit an error"; שָׁגָה means "to wander or go astray, to sin through ignorance", while שָׁגַע means "to be mad, to act or behave like a madman". Sin can occur in any of these ways: ignorance either of the law itself or that a particular action is classed in a certain way; carelessness or inattention, particularly in a moment of stress; being temporarily out of control, either through anger, distress or - literally perhaps - insanity, mental illness or incapacity. Hirsch feels that שָׁגַג is caused by carelessness, so that the person who sins in this way is responsible for not paying proper attention to their actions. "It is just this lack of attention, this carelessness as to whether his actions are in accordance with the demands of the law, wherein lies the sinfulness of his mistake."

Nachmanides is concerned about the effects of even unintentional sin in our lives: "All sins (even if committed unwittingly) produce a particular 'stain' upon the soul and constitute a blemish thereon, and the soul is only worthy to be received by the countenance of its Creator when it is pure of all sin. Were it not so, then all the fools of the world would be deserving to come before Him." He seems to be saying that the smallest infraction, even on a completely ignorant basis or committed by someone who is incapable of understanding or remembering the commandments, is still sin and so requires atonement.

It is important to remember that the Jewish commentators write to the Jewish community, making a basic assumption that all people within the community will have some rudimentary knowledge, or have had at least an opportunity to acquire learning, of the *Torah* and its requirements. Even allowing for Sha'ul and Barnabas' assurance to the people at Lystra that "God has not left Himself without witnesses" (Acts 14:17, NASB) and Rav Sha'ul's letter to the Jewish community in Rome that, "whenever Gentiles, who have no Torah, do naturally what the Torah requires ... their lives show that the conduct the Torah dictates is written within their hearts" (Romans 2:14-15, CJB), we have to make allowance for people raised and brought up without any access to the gospel and those below the age of reason or of diminished responsibility. Rav Sha'ul again: "For the unbelieving husband has been set aside for God by the [believing] wife, and the unbelieving wife has been set aside for God by the brother - otherwise your children would be 'unclean', but as it is, they are set aside for God" (1 Corinthians 7:14, CJB). While this does not mean that the partners and children are 'saved' simply because of their family relationship to a believer, it does create a space and opportunity for people to hear and respond to God's message so that they may acquire the necessary information and act upon it for themselves.

The all-encompassing nature of sin is clearly picked up by James when he wrote to the Jewish people in the *Diaspora* who had come to faith in Yeshua as the Messiah of Israel: "For a person who keeps the whole Torah, yet stumbles at one point, has become guilty of breaking them all" (James 2:10, CJB). James is writing in the context of people who are either saying that some commandments apply and others don't, or who are saying that now they are believers they don't have to do anything at all. James reminds them sharply that "faith by itself, unaccompanied by actions, is dead" (v. 17, CJB); it is the things that we do that demonstrate both to others and to God that our faith is real and that our lives have changed by being in relationship with Him. Whether Jew or Gentile - and there are different specific requirements for both - being a believer has definite obligations. Sin is still sin; disobeying God is sin; Rav Sha'ul wrote, "Heaven forbid! How can we who have died to sin, still live in it?" (Romans 6:2, CJB). John reinforces the situation, then explains God's solution: "If we claim not to have sin, we are deceiving ourselves and the truth is not in us. If we acknowledge our sins, then, since He is trustworthy and just, He will forgive them and purify us from all wrongdoing" (1 John 1:8-9, CJB). Just as a sacrifice was required for even unwitting sin, so as believers every sin must be confessed and brought to God for forgiveness in Yeshua.

Further Study: 2 Kings 22:13; 2 Peter 1:10-11

Application: Are you conscious of having stepped over the line inadvertently and fallen into sin? Know that God wants to bring you out of that situation and has provided from the beginning a way to make that happen. Whether it happened through carelessness, lack of attention or pressure of circumstances, God wants to remove this foothold that sin now has in your life - talk to Him about it today so that you can move on and put it behind you.

וַיִּקְרָא ו׳

Vayikra - And He called - 6

Vayikra / Leviticus 4:27 - 5:10

Vayikra/Leviticus 4:27 And if an individual from among the common people sins unwittingly ...

וְאִם־נֶפֶשׁ אַחַת תֶּחֱטָא בִשְׁגָגָה מֵעַם הָאָרֶץ

ha'aretz mey'am vishgaga tekheta akhat nefesh v'im

The Sages of the Talmud spend some time debating the sin offering that is to be brought in the case of unknowing or inadvertent sin. The word בִשְׁגָגָה, the feminine noun שְׁגָגָה - an unknown or unwitting error - with the prefix preposition בְּ - in - from the root שָׁגַג - to err or commit an error, coupled with the verb תֶּחֱטָא, a 3fs *Qal* prefix form of the verb חָטָא - to miss the mark, fall short, sin - gives the picture of someone who has definitely sinned, but without knowing it, or being aware that they have done so. The next verse says, "if his sin, which he has committed, is made known to him" (v.28, NASB), implying that if a sin remains unknown then, although technically guilty, since the offender doesn't know that he has sinned, the guilt offering is not required since he wouldn't know that he needed to bring one. The Sages concluded that this situation only applies to an offence whose deliberate committal would result in being cut off from the people, but whose unintentional committal required a guilt offering (*b.* Yevamot 9*a*, *b.* Keritot 22*b*, *b.* Horayot 8*a*).

Baruch Levine points out that the phrase עַם הָאָרֶץ - the people of the earth ("common people" above) - is not being used in the derogatory sense that it later came to have by Second Temple times[3] when Peter and John are dismissed by the Pharisees and members of the *Sanhedrin* as simply "uneducated and untrained men" (Acts 4:13, NASB). Levine comments that here, following similar statements about a serving priest (Vayikra 4:3-12), the whole congregation (vv. 13-21) or a leader (vv. 22-26)

---

3. In fact, quite to the contrary, Levine suggests that the *am-ha'aretz* formed a land-owning gentry class that exercised some degree of leadership over Jerusalem and even the country as a whole up until the destruction of the 1st Temple.

sinning inadvertently, this clause is now talking about simply a lay person: someone who is neither a religious professional nor in a leadership role within the community. The Sforno, being aware of the difference between the priests and Levites - those who had education and who were to teach the people the *Torah* - and the people themselves, considers "it is a likely possibility that one of the common people will sin". The religious professionals were considered less likely to sin inadvertently because they were familiar with the *Torah* on a daily basis; the lay people, who were more concerned with agricultural matters and protecting their cities, farms and families, only encountered *Torah* on an occasional basis so might not be aware of all the smaller items and so would naturally be more prone to unintentional sin.

In what might at first appear like nitpicking, the Ba'al HaTurim states[4] that the requirement to bring a sin offering only applies if the sin is performed in its entirety, but not partially. This allows for the position that someone becomes aware of the situation part-way through; by repenting and not finishing off the sinful action, it has not been "done" and so no obligation for a sin offering has been incurred. In the same vein, Hirsch speaks of "the repeated stress which is laid upon a single individual being the bearer of the sin which comes to be atoned for" so pointing us towards the cost of sin to the whole community even if only one individual is involved. Small things repeated many times become habits and build up an atmosphere that is conducive and supportive of sin and others will inevitably question the *Torah* or be drawn into sin themselves. The Sefer HaChinuch says, "It is impracticable for the repentant sinner to cleanse his heart by a mere verbal undertaking to avoid sinning in the future. For this purpose a significant act must be performed, i.e., the sinner must take a he-goat from the sheep-pen and go to the trouble of taking it to the Temple to the *cohen*, where the procedure will be carried out to the last detail, as commanded in the *Torah*."

The issue of continuing sin was obviously something that the early Yeshua-believers also had to deal with. How were they to address habits and lifestyles that they now found - as believers - were not according to God's standards? Rav Sha'ul has to ask, "So then, are we to say, 'Let's keep on sinning, so that there can be more grace'?" (Romans 6:1, CJB). If God's forgiveness was freely available for sin, then some believers might have been suggesting that perhaps a little sin not only wasn't a big deal, but perhaps was also a good thing so that there could be more forgiveness and more for which to thank God. Sha'ul quickly answers his own (rhetorical) question: "Heaven forbid! How can we, who have died to sin, still live in it?" (v. 2, CJB)! He then goes on to show that since we have died and been united

---

4. On the basis of *gematria*.

with Messiah through baptism into His resurrection, we now live in Him; since Yeshua doesn't sin, we should not sin - sin is not to be a part of our resurrected spiritual nature. We have to actualise this in our lives: "In the same way, count yourselves dead to sin but alive to God in Christ Jesus. Therefore do not let sin reign in your mortal body so that you obey its evil desires" (vv. 11-12, NIV). A significant act has taken place in our lives: instead of taking a goat to the *cohen* in the Temple and sacrificing it, so that the procedure not only provides atonement but a very visible and physical deterrent from sin habits, we have met with Yeshua and been "born again"; we have been baptised in His name, we have been set free from the patterns and habits of sin, we have transferred into the Kingdom of God. To use Sha'ul's words again: "having been freed from sin, you became slaves of righteousness" (v. 18, NASB). Now that we belong to God, we are expected to obey the rules of the kingdom and sin, even unintentional sin, is not acceptable behaviour.

In the parable of the Prodigal Son, Yeshua relates the words of the son who - after wasting his inheritance in profligate living - is returning to his father's house, seeking forgiveness and a place among the hired hands. The son says to his father, "Father, I have sinned against Heaven and against you; I am no longer worthy to be called your son" (Luke 15:21, CJB). We repeat the same theme in the words of the general confession:

Father Eternal, Giver of light and grace,
we have sinned against You and against our neighbour,
in what we have thought, in what we have said and done,
through ignorance, through weakness,
through our own deliberate fault.

Whether deliberately, by weak omission or neglect, or simply by not knowing what we should do, as people we sin; as a part of the human race and by the habits of a lifetime, we sooner or later end up sinning - taking decisions quickly, casually, without thinking, that are not in accordance with God's heart. When this happens we need to re-engage with that significant event in our lives; we need to confess our sin to our Father and seek His forgiveness in Yeshua, we need to re-actualise the moment of Calvary in our lives so that we are not only forgiven but changed in a way that makes sin more difficult. Then, cleansed by God on the inside because "If we acknowledge our sins, then, since He is trustworthy and just, He will forgive them and purify us from all wrongdoing" (1 John 1:9, CJB), we count ourselves dead to sin and resolve never to do that again.

Further Study: 1 Kings 8:46-50; Job 33:23-28

Application: Are you frequently tripped up by some besetting sin that seems to grab you again and again, unwittingly or knowingly? God wants to free you from that place, but you have to accept His forgiveness and cleansing to make it a reality in your life. Why not ask Him about this today and put those sinful thoughts and habits behind you once and for all!

וַיִּקְרָא ז'

Vayikra - And He called - 7

Vayikra / Leviticus 5:11 - 26

Vayikra/Leviticus 5:11 ... and if his hand cannot stretch to two turtledoves or to two young doves ...

וְאִם־לֹא תַשִּׂיג יָדוֹ לִשְׁתֵּי תֹרִים אוֹ לִשְׁנֵי

lishney o toriym lishtey yado tasiyg lo v'im

בְּנֵי־יוֹנָה

yonah v'ney

This text offers a number of interesting ideas that should make us think about our relationship with God and the way we see the question of sin. The verse opens by making provision for a person who is too poor to afford the guilt offerings that have been described in the previous verses; as Ibn Ezra comments, someone who is "devoid of possessions". *Targum Onkelos* changes "cannot stretch his hand" to לָא תַדְבֵּק יְדֵיה "his hand does not fall" to show that such a person has nothing to hand, among his immediate possessions or within his reasonable grasp. Known as the sliding scale mechanism, the size of the offering that is required is proportional to the sinner's ability to pay. The sacrifice must be meaningful, but not unattainable. Chizkuni makes the point that the offender "is not required to borrow in order to bring a more expensive offering." Richard Elliott Friedman makes the telling comment that "a person is not to be prevented from getting atonement because of lack of money." It is not *HaShem's* intention that anyone should be unable to restore their relationship with Him; on the contrary, the levels are set so that they are appropriate for each range of income and position within society. No-one is excluded and everyone can make atonement for their sin.

The verse ends with the phrase, "he shall not place oil on it, nor shall he put frankincense on it, for it is a sin offering". Rashi comments "and it is not proper that the offering be splendid", based on Rabbi Simeon's teaching: "By right the sinner's meal-offering should require oil and frankincense, so that the sinner should have no advantage (by being spared the cost of those ingredients); why then does it not require them? In order that his offering be not sumptuous" (*b*. Menachot 6*a*). The guilt offering is a response to various kinds of both deliberate and inadvertent sin; when the offender becomes aware that he has sinned, he must bring a guilt offering to rectify the situation. It should therefore be a plain and simple offering, unadorned or dressed up in any way. The same austerity can be seen in the offering brought in the case of a woman suspected of adultery (B'Midbar 5:15). As Nahum Sarna comments, "It was thought that God took no delight in receiving such offerings and would have preferred, so to speak, that they had not been necessary in the first place!"

Yeshua spoke directly into these situations when He taught what are known as the parables of the Kingdom. Found only in Matthew's gospel, they go like this: "The Kingdom of Heaven is like a treasure hidden in a field. A man found it, hid it again, then in great joy went and sold everything he owned, and bought that field. Again, the Kingdom of Heaven is like a merchant on the lookout for fine pearls. On finding one very valuable pearl he went away, sold everything he owned and bought it" (Matthew 13:44-46, CJB). The pattern of telling two parables together, back to back, is a common technique that Yeshua used in His teaching; they are referred to as "partner parables". On some occasions the parables have been split up in the gospel records, on many others they have remained together.

The first parable concerns a treasure hidden in a field. We are not given the background or the exact circumstances of the find - they are not interesting - we are simply told that it is found by a man who does not own the field. Kistemaker comments, "We are not told what the treasure was, but the man was dumb-founded. He had never seen such a valuable treasure before. It could be his if he owned the field." He quickly hides the treasure by burying it and negotiates to purchase the field. But he has a problem: the price! To buy the field will cost everything that he has. In order to make the purchase, he has to sell everything else that he owned. His knowledge of the value of the treasure makes this worthwhile and - perhaps to the amazement of his friends and neighbours - he completes the transaction and rejoices with great joy.

The second parable, although similar, is slightly different; this time the focus is on the man rather than the treasure. The man is looking for pearls - a commodity of no small value, then as now - and in the course of his normal business transactions, examining and inspecting merchandise, he finds a pearl that he instantly recognises as being outstanding. Even to an experienced merchant, dealing with run-of-the-mill pearls every day, this pearl was exceptional. He does not have enough money with him to buy the pearl, so he goes away to perform some calculations and make sure that he can meet the price being demanded. Once he is sure, he too sells everything that he has and returns to purchase the pearl of great price, "the sort of pearl that dealers dream of getting their hands on." (Wenham) Obviously, the means of a man working in a field, perhaps on day-work, and the means of a merchant routinely dealing in pearls, will be significantly different. Yet both give everything they have - and it is enough in both cases - to complete their purchase and own the item of desire.

Brad Young asks, "What price must the disciple be willing to pay? When he or she decides to answer the challenging call of Yeshua, the cost involves everything he or she owns, as well as all relationships with other people. How is it possible, on the other hand, to measure the worth of God's reign? The kingdom is infinitely beyond human value, but these parables teach that the kingdom is within one's grasp if one is willing to sacrifice all to obtain it." The Rabbis have connected the pearl with *Torah* learning and used similar parables to depict the relationship between God and Israel, but the common thread of both parables is the passion of the finder to make the purchase. It is not simply that the treasure or pearl has a large price; or even that however high the price may be, it is affordable by everyone who is committed to paying it. Rather, it is that the finder of the treasure, the merchant who found the pearl, sold everything, left no stone unturned, withheld nothing, in order to secure the item. Their passion and joy in pushing through family objections, social mores, the practical difficulties of realising that amount of money, to complete the purchase, was what enabled them to reach their goal and fully enter in to the Kingdom of Heaven.

So for the poor man who cannot afford a sheep or a goat, or even a pair of turtledoves or pigeons, a simple offering of flour is enough to restore relationship with God. But the offering must be unadorned, undecorated, with all the value contained in the offering itself so that nothing is for show but all is for God. Atonement must be affordable by all, but stretch everyone to their limit so that God is certain of being everything in their lives. We must not only accept Yeshua as our Saviour but fully invest in Him to make Him Lord in our lives as well. Only then will we be able to fully enter the Kingdom of Heaven.

Further Study: 2 Corinthians 8:9; Proverbs 23:23; Revelation 3:18

Application: Where do you stand in the Kingdom of God? Have you fully invested your life and know that you now own that pearl of great price, or have you offered only a token and remain unsure whether you have been accepted or not? Perhaps it is time to review your portfolio and determine where your assets are for "where your treasure is, there will your heart be also" (Matthew 6:21, NASB).

צַו

Tzav - Command

Vayikra / Leviticus 6:1 - 8:36

רִאשׁוֹן	Aliyah One	Vayikra/Leviticus 6:1 - 11
שֵׁנִי	Aliyah Two	Vayikra/Leviticus 6:12 - 7:10
שְׁלִישִׁי	Aliyah Three	Vayikra/Leviticus 7:11 - 38
רְבִיעִי	Aliyah Four	Vayikra/Leviticus 8:1 - 13
חֲמִשִׁי	Aliyah Five	Vayikra/Leviticus 8:14 - 21
שִׁשִׁי	Aliyah Six	Vayikra/Leviticus 8:22 - 29
שְׁבִיעִי	Aliyah Seven	Vayikra/Leviticus 8:30 - 36

צַו א׳

Tzav - Command - 1

Vayikra / Leviticus 6:1 - 11

Vayikra/Leviticus 6:2 Give this order to Aharon and his sons, "This is the law for the burnt offering ..."

צַו אֶת־אַהֲרֹן וְאֶת־בָּנָיו לֵאמֹר זֹאת תּוֹרַת הָעֹלָה
ha'olah   torat   zot   leymor banayv v'et   Aharon   et tzav

The Sages of the Talmud tell us that when the *Torah* uses צַו, command, rather than דִּבֵּר, speak, or אָמֹר, say, it indicates three things: (a) an urging on, (b) that the command must be carried out immediately and, (c) it must also be performed by future generations (*b. Kiddushin 29a*). Perhaps we should ask why this level of stress is needed for the laws of the burnt offering. Rashi points out that the *Tanna* Rabbi Shimon said, "Scripture must especially urge in a situation where there is a loss of money". In order to serve in the Temple, the priests had to leave their normal occupations to come to Jerusalem. With the other animal offerings, the *cohanim* got both meat and the hides, whereas with the burnt offering, only the hide is given to the priests. This would make the offering of a burnt offering less financially rewarding than the other types of offerings, so the Sages tell us that Aharon and his sons are specifically urged to carry out this duty as well as the rest of their functions.

This may be why Rav Sha'ul write to Titus saying, "speak confidently, so that those who have believed God may be careful to engage in good deeds" (Titus 3:8, NASB), or "... may apply themselves to doing good deeds" (CJB). When there are a number of things that need to be done, or can be done, at the same time, we often choose first those which please us most or offer the most reward - be that spiritually or financially - leaving the less pleasant or attractive things until later, hoping that someone else might do them before we get back. After all, if they need doing, surely it doesn't matter if we pick the ones which we prefer; we then rationalise our choice by reasoning that those particular tasks suit us best, they are a better fit with our skill set or calling, so we will naturally do them better than other people whose skills lie in those other areas.

Yeshua spent one *Shabbat* at the home of a leading Pharisee (Luke 14:1-11) and noticed that the guests were choosing the best seats at the table. He cautioned them in a story to beware of picking out the best place because that may have been reserved for someone else: "instead, when you are invited, go and sit in the least important place; so that when the one who invited you comes, he will say to you, 'Go on up to a better seat'" (Luke 14:10, CJB). Like Aharon and his sons, we need to make sure that all the jobs get done without picking and choosing those which we would 'like' to do.

Further Study: Ephesians 2:8-10; James 1:26-27

Application: Have you been focusing on only some of the things that the Lord has given you to do, to the neglect of other equally important but less attractive things? If so, then why not take this opportunity to apologise and catch up on some of the other stuff.

צַו

צֵו 'ב

Tzav - Command - 2

Vayikra / Leviticus 6:12 - 7:10

Vayikra/Leviticus 6:13 This is the offering of Aharon and his sons that each shall offer to Adonai on the day he is initiated ... continually

זֶה קׇרְבַּן אַהֲרֹן וּבָנָיו אֲשֶׁר־יַקְרִיבוּ לַיהוה

l'Adonai yak'riyvu asher oovanayv Aharon korban zeh

בְּיוֹם הִמָּשַׁח אֹתוֹ ... תָּמִיד

tamiyd ... oto himashakh b'yom

Rashi was neither the first nor the last to comment on the apparent contradiction in this text: is this offering made once upon the day of first taking office, or is it a continuous offering? The Sages spent some time on the issue (*b.* Menachot 51*b*) and Rashi concludes that this grain offering was brought once in his career by an ordinary priest, when he first starts officiating in the sanctuary and every day by the *Cohen Gadol*, High Priest - those sons of Aharon who succeed him in that office. Hirsch adds that "The High Priest, on the day of his entry into that office, has to bring the offering twice and if he was appointed High Priest before being active as an ordinary priest, he would have brought it three times" (cf. *b.* Menachot 78*a*). This can be seen as a symbol of availability: the regular priests served in turns - later to be set in a rota by King David (1 Chronicles 24) - whereas the High Priest was technically 'on duty' every day, to supervise the work of the priests, use the *Urim* and *Thumim* and be the visible intermediary between God and the people.

Access to and availability of one's gods was a serious issue in the ancient world. Greek and Roman myths about their gods are full of stories that illustrate not only how fickle they were, but how often they were not available: on journeys, at parties, asleep, fighting or simply living their own lives. The prophet Elijah taunted the prophets of Ba'al, "Call a little louder - maybe he's off meditating somewhere or other, or maybe he's got involved in a project, or maybe he's on vacation. You don't suppose he's overslept, do you, and needs to be woken up?" (1 Kings 18:27-28, The Message). The Psalmist portrays the opposite picture of the God of Israel: "He who keeps you will not slumber. Behold, He who keeps Israel will neither slumber nor sleep" (Psalm 121:3-4, NASB). Our God is never asleep or 'off-duty'. He is always available to protect and guard His people, to stop them slipping or stumbling, and to preserve them as His witnesses.

In the book of Hebrews, the writer expounds the virtues of Yeshua as the great High Priest. As believers, we are urged to "draw near with confidence to the throne of grace, that we may receive mercy and may find grace to help in times of need" (Hebrews 4:16, NASB). He is available on a 24 x 7 basis for all those who trust in Him for help, encouragement, support and companionship. As the writer goes on to say, "He is able to save forever those who drawn near to God through Him, since He always lives to make intercession for them" (7:25, NASB). Yeshua made the one perfect sacrifice (10:12) when He took up office - and now serves as our perfect intermediary (1 Timothy 2:5) between Father God and His people, continually, always, for ever. Yeshua Himself echoed Moshe's words, "He will never leave you or forsake you" (D'varim 31:6, KJV), when He said, "I will be with you always, yes, even until the end of the age" (Matthew 28:20, CJB).

Further Study: Psalm 118:5-14; Matthew 18:19-20

Application: When things get tough, it is all too easy to think that God has forsaken us and is just leaving us to get on with it. Nothing could be further from the truth. It is when things are toughest that Yeshua is closest to us, just waiting for us to cry out to Him. Try it today!

צַו גּ׳

Tzav - Command - 3

Vayikra / Leviticus 7:11 - 38

Vayikra/Leviticus 7:11 And this is the law of the peace-offering that he will bring to Adonai

וְזֹאת תּוֹרַת זֶבַח הַשְּׁלָמִים אֲשֶׁר יַקְרִיו לַיהוה׃

la'Adonai yak'riyv asher hash'lamiym zevakh torat v'zot

Our sages talk about the peace-offerings. "Rabbi Yehudah said: Whoever brings שְׁלָמִים, peace-offerings, brings שָׁלוֹם, peace, into the world. Another explanation: It harbours 'peace' for all parties; the blood and inwards parts - for the altar, the breast and shoulder - for the priests, the skin and meat - for the owners" (Sifra 156). There is an inherent word-play involved here, for the word שָׁלוֹם does not only mean 'peace' but also 'wholeness' or 'completeness', so that the picture of the peace-offering is that it is a means of bringing wholeness or completeness as a part of thanksgiving.

Rashi gives a set of examples of when a peace-offering should be brought - particularly thank-offerings: "over a miracle that was done for him, for example seafarers, and those who travel deserts, those who were confined in prison, and a sick person who was healed, for they must give thanks." These may have been life-threatening events, or at least significantly traumatic seasons in the lives of people. So, Rashi says, they are to bring a peace-offering to thank God for preserving them. But there is more to it than that. It is not just that they bring the offering to thank God, but that in the process they are giving closure to the trauma; by making the offering they receive peace - this is a completion ritual that marks the end of the episode, even if the point of stress has already passed, so that the mind can mark that chapter as closed and move on. Peace, equilibrium, has been restored. The offering not only thanks God and makes a public statement attributing preservation to God, but also acts as an anchor to declare the end of the storm and set everyone back on an even keel.

Rav Sha'ul writes, "For it was the Father's good pleasure ... to reconcile all things to Himself, having made peace through the blood of His cross"

(Colossians 1:19-20, NASB). Here we see Yeshua not only being our sin offering but our peace offering; not only taking away our sin, but bringing closure to our past life containing that sin, sealing it off as a closed chapter in our lives and setting us off again on a level playing field. "But now, you who were once far off have been brought near through the shedding of Messiah's blood. For He Himself is our shalom, our peace" (Ephesians 2:13-14, CJB). Not only did He, once for all, at a point in history, become our peace offering reconciling us to God, but He continues to be our peace offering now. Yeshua is our peace offering every day, bringing closure to the mistakes and sin that - being human - we make each day. Every day He brings us peace and wholeness, setting us back on the level before Father God. This is why He said to the *talmidim*, "What I am leaving you with is shalom - I am giving My shalom ... Don't let yourselves be upset or frightened" (John 14:27, CJB).

Further Study: Psalm 34:12-14; Isaiah 27:2-5; Hebrews 12:14-16

Application: Are you at peace, or are you always on edge, always looking over your shoulder as if someone or something is pursuing you? If so, then you need to know God's peace for, as the Rabbis say, "All offerings will be abolished, except the thanksgiving offering" (Vayikra Rabbah 9,2).

צַו

Tzav - Command - 4

Vayikra / Leviticus 8:1 - 13

Vayikra/Leviticus 8:2 Take Aharon and his sons with him ...

קַח אֶת־אַהֲרֹן וְאֶת־בָּנָיו אִתּוֹ

ito banayv v'et Aharon et kakh

With the start of chapter 8, the narrative in the book of Vayikra resumes, to recount the ordination of Aharon as the *Cohen Gadol*, High Priest, in accordance with the instructions God has given Moshe. At this point, Rashi makes the comment: "this section of the *Torah* was said seven days before the erection of the *Mishkan*, for there is no earlier and later in the *Torah*." In other words, Rashi is saying that the events in the *Torah* are not presented in chronological sequence. This position is strongly denied by the Ramban: "Why should we invert the words of the Living God! Rather, the correct interpretation is ...."

The source of the dissent is found at the end of the previous book of the *Torah*: "Now it came about in the first month of the second year, on the first day of the month, that the tabernacle was erected" (Shemot 40:17, NASB), followed by the detailed steps of erection and placement, "Thus Moshe finished the work" (v.33, NASB), and *HaShem* gave His sign of approval: "Then the cloud covered the tent of meeting, and the glory of Adonai filled the tabernacle" (v.34, NASB) in just the same way that *HaShem* took up residence hundreds of years later in the Temple built by Solomon (2 Chronicles 7:1-2). The essence of the dispute is that the earlier narrative places the presence of God filling the *Mishkan* on the day that Moshe erected it, whereas the latter narrative (see 9:23 in the next portion, *Shemini*) leaves the descent of the cloud until after the seven days of Aharon's inauguration.

Rashi solves the problem by time-shifting this section of the text back to before Shemot chapter 40, and thus concluding that the *Torah* does not always present things in the order that they actually happened. By his reckoning, these instructions were given seven days before the erection of the tabernacle so that the instructions preceded any of the enactment.

31

Ramban tackles the issue by proposing that the tabernacle was actually erected seven days earlier, on the 23rd Adar, followed by these instructions, but that the formal "opening" of the tabernacle was on the 1st Nissan when Aharon had been inaugurated - in other words that the tabernacle could not fully function without the *Cohen Gadol* to serve in it, so that although it was erected and being used for the inauguration it was not formally operational until the seven days had passed.

What are Rashi and the Ramban doing here? Are they completely mad to be arguing so heatedly over such an issue? Does it really matter? At the same time that these two rabbis are debating this, Christian theologians were having exactly the same arguments resolving the gospel narratives and trying to establish a clear chronology of the life and ministry of Yeshua. Although the particular subject material is different, the process and the motivation for it are exactly the same: to show that apparent inconsistencies can have reasonable explanations and so to prove or demonstrate the integrity of the Scripture. Faith must have reason and balance on its side; we are not called to believe nonsense!

Does it really matter that Matthew and Luke often tell different stories about Yeshua, or the same stories in a different order? To a critic who is looking to avoid taking the claims of Yeshua seriously, the differences provide an excuse for discrediting the gospels and so being able to ignore them. To those with an open mind, those same differences confirm the validity and integrity of the texts by demonstrating them to be largely independent and eye-witness accounts; their differences show that the authors did not collude or plan together at the time of writing and neither has the church orchestrated a massive conspiracy afterwards to fabricate the gospel narratives.

And what is that to us? Simply that we too must be engaged in being sure of our faith, not just relying on the work of professional theologians and apologeticists. As Rav Sha'ul told Timothy, "Study to show yourself approved before God, a workman that need not be ashamed, rightly dividing the word of truth" (2 Timothy 2:15, KJV). We must be like the Bereans who "were very willing to receive God's message, and every day they carefully examined the Scriptures to see if what Sha'ul said was true" (Acts 17:11, GWT).

Further Study: Psalm 1:1-3; 2 Timothy 3:14-15

Application: If you wonder sometimes about the ordering and content of the Bible, then take heart: you are not alone, many others have so wondered. Be encouraged to keep reading and studying, to apply your mind to the matter and ask God to confirm the truth of His word and show you resources that will enable your faith to be built up and informed.

צַו ה'

Tzav - Command - 5

Vayikra / Leviticus 8:14 - 21

Vayikra/Leviticus 8:14 And he brought forward the bull of the sin offering

וַיַּגֵּשׁ אֵת פַּר הַחַטָּאת
ha'khatat   par   eyt   vayageysh

The verb that starts this clause, וַיַּגֵּשׁ, is a *Hif'il* prefix 3ms form of the verb נָגַשׁ in a *vav*-conversive construct. The root means "to draw or come near, to approach" (Davidson) and would normally have a preposition - such as to, in, on, over - to indicate the target of the movement. In *Hif'il*, however, the causative meaning is "to bring near, to offer or present" and allows the grammar to omit the indirect object, as here. No doubt the animal in question was distinctly uneasy, so that a measure of coercion would be required to bring it forward to the front of the crowd for Aharon and his sons to lay their hands upon it and Moshe to slaughter it. Levine points out that "large cattle were used in sin offerings associated with purification when the entire community and the High Priest, in particular, were affected." This can also be seen at the start of the *Yom Kippur* ritual where Aharon offers a bull for his own sins and those of his household (cf. Vayikra 16).

Also visible in this verse and the little block that follows is the degree of obedience to the instructions given for this procedure in Shemot 29:10-14, that prescribe how the installation of the High Priest is to be performed. One can see, too, the similarity to the ritual described in Vayikra 4:3-12 to be employed if a priest needs to bring a sin offering. Today Moshe officiates, from tomorrow onwards Aharon and his sons will officiate as the installed and anointed priests. Everything is done according to the instructions, following the pattern set down and ordained by God. Nothing is added or omitted; no one deviates from the divine order so that the process may be approved and accepted by God. When two of Aharon's sons depart from the plan by their own innovation, as chapter 10 tragically tells us, God acts to protect His holiness and preserve the divine initiative and procedure in the sequence of worship and approach to His presence.

These verses, then, are a detailed and intricate record of explicit obedience to God's commandments. The *Torah* takes the time and space to preserve the record because it is important that future generations should understand exactly how things were done. It is all the more surprising to find God speaking hundreds of years later through the prophets, in this week's *Haftarah* portion, concerning this process. "Add your burnt offerings to your sacrifices and eat the flesh. For in the day that I brought them out of the land of Egypt, I did not speak to your fathers or command them concerning burnt offerings and sacrifices" (Jeremiah 7:21-22, RSV). He didn't? What have we been reading so far in the book of Vayikra if it isn't detailed and explicit commands about burnt offerings and sacrifices? How are we to understand these startling words from Jeremiah - can he really be speaking from God? Isn't the precise execution of ritual the focus of God's heart? Jeremiah goes on: "But this command I gave them, 'Obey My voice, and I will be your God, and you will be my people; and walk in all the way that I command you, that it may go well with you'" (v. 23, RSV).

We seem to have a contradiction here: either God did or did not command the people to obey Him. Perhaps the words of Isaiah, spoken a few years earlier, will help to clarify what is going on here. "Bring your worthless offerings no longer, incense is an abomination to Me ... I hate your new moon festivals and your appointed feasts, they have become a burden to Me" (Isaiah 1:13-14, NASB). These are strong words from the God who established and set up the feasts and new moon rituals in the first place - what is Isaiah saying? The following verse explains: "your hands are covered with blood" (v15, NASB). Not the blood of the sacrifices, but the blood of the oppressed: "Wash yourselves, make yourselves clean; remove the evil of your deeds from My sight. Cease to do evil, learn to do good; seek justice, reprove the ruthless; defend the orphan, plead for the widow" (v. 16-17, NASB). The remedy to the situation lay entirely in the hands of the people; by changing their behaviour, by observing God's commandments, they could bring about restoration. Why? Because the real focus of God's commandments was about the behaviour of the people: being compassionate and caring for the disadvantaged, being honest in business and honouring God in their conduct and relationships. The sacrificial system only provided a way of covering over sin and atoning for one's mistakes, a mechanism for approaching God and confessing shortcomings in a way that expressed their cost or value both to the individual and the community, as well as visibly demonstrating God's acceptance of the people and the restoration of peace and relationship.

Yeshua goes right to the heart of the matter in one of His late discourses with the Scribes and Pharisees. "Woe to you hypocritical Torah-teachers and P'rushim! You pay your tithes of mint, dill and cumin; but you have neglected the weightier matters of the Torah - justice, mercy, trust. These are things you should have attended to - without neglecting the others! Blind guides! - straining out a gnat, meanwhile swallowing a camel!" (Matthew 23:23-24, CJB). Like all people, the Pharisees had become bogged down in the minutiae - the small stuff - so that they had taken their eyes off the larger picture and lost the context in which tithing was to take place. The tithing - and recognising God's concern about the small corners of our lives - is not in itself disapproved of by Yeshua; on the contrary, He affirms the Pharisees' details while trying to pull their noses back from the brickwork to have them see the whole wall and the building to which it belongs.

Further Study: Hosea 6:6; Amos 5:21-24; John 13:17

Application: Have you lost sight of the larger picture of what God wants to do in your life and in the Body of Messiah around you? It is all too easy to become absorbed in our immediate patch of detail and so miss the cries of help, the shouts of blessings, the tears of mourning and shrieks of laughter all around us that *HaShem* wants us to be a part of. Pull back today, come up for air and ask God to show you the larger picture around your life.

צַו

Tzav - Command - 6

Vayikra / Leviticus 8:22 - 29

Vayikra/Leviticus 8:22 And [Moshe] brought near the second ram, the ram of ordination

וַיַּקְרֵב אֶת־הָאַיִל הַשֵּׁנִי אֵיל הַמִּלֻּאִים

hamiluiym   eyl   hasheniy ha'ayil   et   vayakreyv

The word הַמִּלֻּאִים attracts some attention as it is not the word that might be expected at this point. *Targum Onkelos*, indeed, replaces it with קֻרְבָּנַיָּא - literally, sacrifice - a word taken from Sifra; *Onkelos* is perhaps trying "to capture the essence of a symbolic ceremonial act that initiates or confers office or status" (Drazin & Wagner). Rashi, pointing to the literal meaning of the word says, "**The ram of ordination**: the ram of the peace offering for מִלּוּאִים - literally 'fillings' - expresses שְׁלָמִים - 'peace offerings' or 'completenesses' - for they fill and complete the *cohanim* in their priesthood." The root מָלֵא - to be full, filled; to be fulfilled, completed; to fill, make full - is being compared to the overlapping meanings of the root שָׁלֵם - to be completed, finished; to be at peace. The ritual, described below in verses 27-29 completes the official transfer of role and authority to the incoming priests: in this case Aharon and his sons, in the future, successive generations of both high and ordinary priests. The Ramban, citing the instructions for this ceremony given in Shemot 29:1, explains that "the second ram is specifically called the ram of ordination, because it was the last of the offerings, and it was after that that their consecration was complete and they ministered before Him, blessed be He, for all these offerings were indispensable in the matter."

Levine points out that "the biblical formula מִלֵּא יָד - to fill the hand - is limited to the appointment of priests and cultic officials." The formula - usually translated 'consecrate' - is found elsewhere in the narrative texts; a young Levite from Bethlehem agrees to be the family priest of a landowner in the hills of Ephraim for a stipend and "after Mikhah consecrated the Levi, the young man became his cohen and stayed there in Mikhah's house" (Judges

17:12, CJB). Similarly, when King Jereboam was establishing the kingdom of Israel and felt that he needed to break the link between the worship of God and the temple in Jerusalem, he "appointed priests for the high places from all sorts of people. Anyone who wanted to become a priest he consecrated for the high places" (1 Kings 13:33, NIV). When Ezekiel was describing his vision of the temple and the instructions God gave him for its construction and consecration, he wrote "For seven days they shall make atonement for the altar and purify it; so shall they consecrate it. And when they have completed the days, it shall be that on the eighth day and onward, the priests shall offer your burnt offerings on the altar, and your peace offerings; and I will accept you,' declares the Lord God" (Ezekiel 43:26-27, NASB).

The story of Yeshua's ministry begins with such an event. While not a formal sacrifice offered in the temple, Yeshua comes to the Jordan to be baptised by John the Immerser. After a brief argument about protocol: "Yochanan tried to stop him. 'You are coming to me? I ought to be immersed by you!' However, Yeshua answered him, 'Let it be this way now, because we should do everything righteousness requires'" (Matthew 3:14-15, CJB), the text tells us that "While all the people were being immersed, Yeshua too was immersed. As He was praying, heaven was opened; the Ruach HaKodesh came down on Him in physical form like a dove; and a voice came from heaven, 'You are My Son, whom I love; I am well pleased with you'" (Luke 3:21-22, CJB); Yeshua was being "filled" for His ministry, His time of service to God. In this case, it was not simply Yeshua's hands that were being filled but His whole life and body being "completed" to empower and enable Him to perform the healing and other attesting miracles that authenticated His ministry, to equip Him to preach and teach the word and way of God and, ultimately, to endure arrest, trial, beating and execution on the stake. It was that life and power that brought the victory: "God raised Him from the dead, freeing Him from the agony of death, because it was impossible for death to keep its hold on Him" (Acts 2:24, NIV).

The writer to the Hebrews takes the theme further: "In bringing many sons to glory, it was fitting that God, for whom and through whom everything exists, should make the author of their salvation perfect through suffering" (Hebrews 2:10, NIV). Should we assume from this that Yeshua was less than perfect before the cross? No, the same principle is at work in this text: the experience of suffering at Calvary "filled the hands" of Yeshua and marked Him as consecrated for the unique ministry He has as our Mediator, our High Priest and our Atonement. Rav Sha'ul is even more explicit concerning his own ministry: "Now I rejoice in my sufferings for your sake, and in my flesh I do my share on behalf of His body (which is the church) in filling up that which is lacking in Christ's afflictions" (Colossians 1:24, NASB). Can Sha'ul possibly be saying that Yeshua's afflictions - carried out to bring about our reconciliation with Father God - are incomplete or insufficient for the task? No, he carefully chooses the words "filling up" to show that he too is using the same word picture of ordination or consecration; by the sufferings and hardships that he is undertaking in travelling and spreading the gospel through the Mediterranean world - the Jewish communities and Gentiles whom he meets along the way - Sha'ul is pointing to the consecration of Yeshua as the Saviour of both Jew and Gentile in a way that Yeshua's own ministry did not do, geographically confined as it was to Israel. By his exertions within the body of Messiah, Sha'ul is reaching people and places that Yeshua Himself could not do on a natural level, although of course He is speaking and working through Sha'ul in both words and miracles.

Are we also to be involved in this process? Absolutely! Peter tells us, "Beloved, do not be surprised at the fiery ordeal among you, which comes upon you for your testing, as though some strange thing were happening to you; but to the degree that you share the sufferings of Christ, keep on rejoicing; so that also at the revelation of His glory, you may rejoice with exultation" (1 Peter 4:12-13, NASB). As believers we should expect to play our part in consecrating - setting apart, declaring holy - Yeshua and sharing the accompanying suffering: misunderstanding, rejection, being laughed at and, in some cases, persecution. How are we to survive this testing and still serve God? The answer is still the same: be filled. Rav Sha'ul again: "Don't get drunk with wine, because it makes you lose control. Instead, keep on being filled with the Spirit - sing psalms, hymns and spiritual songs to each other; sing to the Lord and make music in your heart to Him; always give thanks for everything to God the Father in the name of our Lord Yeshua the Messiah" (Ephesians 5:18-20, CJB). It is as we are filled by the Spirit of God, the Holy Spirit, that we are enabled to witness for God; not only do we consecrate Yeshua as the Messiah but we are ourselves consecrated in the process, becoming like Him.

It is as we hunger for Him and come to Him on a daily basis that He meets with us and fills our hands; He sets us apart that we may set Him apart by our words, our actions and our lives. That is what He promised for each of us: "How blessed are you who are hungry! for you will be filled" (Luke 6:21, CJB).

Further Study: Psalm 63:3-5; Isaiah 55:1-3; Luke 11:33

Application: Are you empty and dry? Do you long to see God moving in power? Today is the time to bring forward the ram of ordination - yourself - so that Yeshua may fill you with His Spirit and consecrate you for the service of the kingdom. Experience fullness and completion as you fill His hands so that He may fill yours.

צַו

צַו ז׳

Tzav - Command - 7

Vayikra / Leviticus 8:30 - 36

Vayikra/Leviticus 8:30 And Moshe took from the oil of the anointing and from the blood ... and he sanctified Aharon ...

וַיִּקַּח מֹשֶׁה מִשֶּׁמֶן הַמִּשְׁחָה וּמִן־הַדָּם ...

... hadam umin hamishkhah mishemen Moshe vayikakh

וַיְקַדֵּשׁ אֶת־אַהֲרֹן

Aharon et vaykadeysh

Both שֶׁמֶן - oil - and הַדָּם - the blood - are singular nouns. As a rule, the word blood is usually singular when referring to animal blood, but plural when describing human blood, as for example דְּמֵי אָחִיךָ - your brother's blood - Abel's blood that cried out from the ground (B'resheet 4:10). In this case, the blood is from the burnt offering (Vayikra 8:19) and the inauguration offering (8:24) that had been thrown on the altar. Nachmanides alerts us to the interesting observation that things seem to be out of order here in the account of what happened when compared to the instructions that Moshe had been given. Back in the book of Shemot, before the Tabernacle had been constructed, Moshe was told how to inaugurate Aharaon and his sons as priests: "Then you shall take some of the blood that is on the altar and some of the anointing oil, and sprinkle it on Aaron and on his garments, and on his sons and on his sons' garments with him; so he and his garments shall be consecrated, as well as his sons and his sons' garments with him" (Shemot 29:21, NASB), before the mention of the inauguration ram, whereas our text has it happening after the inauguration ram has been slaughtered and its blood poured on the altar. Nachmanides comments, "Moshe deduced that these sprinklings were the last things to be done to them, through which they would become completely holy ... thus he completed the sanctification by means of these sprinklings."

The *Torah* contains several images of sprinkling things with blood to "consecrate" them or make them holy. The people, for example, are sprinkled with blood when they and Moshe ratify the covenant: "So Moshe took the blood and sprinkled it on the people, and said, 'Behold the blood of the covenant, which the Lord has made with you in accordance with all these words'" (Shemot 24:8, NASB). Israel is instructed to consecrate the priests, "You shall consecrate him, therefore, for he offers the bread of your God; he shall be holy to you; for I the Lord, who sanctifies you, am holy" (Vayikra 21:8, NASB), so that they may be holy for the people in the same way as *HaShem* Himself is holy. The people are even to consecrate themselves, "You shall consecrate yourselves therefore and be holy, for I am the Lord your God" (Vayikra 20:7, NASB) because *HaShem* is their God and is to dwell among them. This is also because Israel are a sign people, set apart from all the other nations of the world as a witness to *HaShem*: "Thus you are to be holy to Me, for I the Lord am holy; and I have set you apart from the peoples to be Mine" (Vayikra 20:26, NASB).

It is not, however, just sprinkling that makes Israel and the priests holy, it is specifically sprinkling with blood. This is because blood represents life, the shed life of a sacrifice, and brings atonement. "For the life of the flesh is in the blood, and I have given it to you on the altar to make atonement for your souls; for it is the blood by reason of the life that makes atonement" (Vayikra 17:11, NASB). This remains so on an ongoing basis; even today, every sin that is committed requires a blood sacrifice to atone for it. So much so that the writer to the Hebrew confirms that "according to the Law ... all things are cleansed with blood, and without shedding of blood there is no forgiveness" (Hebrews 9:22, NASB). But for nearly two thousand years there has been no temple and no ritually clean priests and Levites to offer sacrifices - how can we find our atonement or be consecrated?

God has provided a way for Jew and Gentile alike to enter into relationship with Him. Rav Sha'ul writes: "Praised be Adonai, Father of our Lord Yeshua the Messiah, who in the Messiah has blessed us with every spiritual blessing in heaven. In the Messiah He chose us in love before the creation of the universe to be holy and without defect in His presence" (Ephesians 1:3-4, CJB). Not only has God provided a way to enter that relationship, it is His purpose that we should be holy - consecrated, set apart - before Him; that is why He chose us: in love and before this world was even created. The Apostle Peter, quoting one of the commands that God gave in the *Torah*, echoes Sha'uls's words: "like the Holy One who called you, be holy yourselves also in all your behavior; because it is written, 'You shall be holy, for I am holy'" (1 Peter 1:15-16, NASB). What God calls people to do, He also enables them to do; there is no command without empowerment, for God's attribute of justice forbids that He should give a command that cannot be fulfilled. The writer to the Hebrews explains how this works: "For when every commandment had been spoken by Moshe to all the people according to the Law, he took the blood of the calves and the goats, with water and scarlet wool and hyssop, and sprinkled both the book itself and all the people, saying,

'This is the blood of the covenant which God commanded you' ... Therefore Yeshua also, that He might sanctify the people through His own blood, suffered outside the gate" (Hebrews 9:19-20, 13:12, NASB). After Moshe gave our people all the commandments, he sanctified them by sprinkling them with the blood. In the same way, Yeshua, provided a sprinkling of His blood to provide atonement and sanctification for us.

While Moshe performed the sprinkling at Sinai, after he had received the *Torah* and shared it with the people, Yeshua goes back one stage to the moment of liberation. The people of Israel were liberated on the 14th Aviv, the night of the Passover, when they daubed the blood on the lintels and doorposts of their houses so that the destroyer - who killed all the firstborn in Egypt - would not enter. At the annual celebration of that event, the Passover *seder* that Yeshua kept with His *talmidim*, He used the ritual of the meal to announce the critical change that His imminent death and resurrection would bring about. Four cups of wine are drunk during the *Seder*; one each to remember the four great promises that God spoke to Moshe just before the event: "I **will free you** from the forced labor of the Egyptians, **rescue you** from their oppression, and **redeem you** with an outstretched arm and with great judgments. I **will take you as My people**, and I will be your God" (Shemot 6:6-7, CJB, emphasis added). Yeshua used the cup after the meal, the third of the four cups of wine, to pick up on the third promise - "I **will redeem you**" as the gospel narrative makes clear: "He did the same with the cup after the meal, saying, 'This cup is the New Covenant, ratified by My blood, which is being poured out for you'" (Luke 22:20, CJB).

Moshe, then, sanctified Aharon and his sons by sprinkling them with oil - a symbol for the Holy Spirit - and blood. Yeshua ratified the covenant that Moshe foretold by shedding His own blood (and water, remember the spear thrust into His side that produced blood and water (John 19:34)), so that John could write, "He is the one who came by means of water and blood, Yeshua the Messiah - not with water only, but with the water and the blood" (1 John 5:6, CJB). Water is also a symbol for the Spirit, so that John can conclude the verse, "And the Spirit bears witness, because the Spirit is the truth". We must all make sure that we hear the witness of the *Ruach Elohim* and celebrate our atonement and sanctification in Messiah Yeshua.

Further Study: Isaiah 53:7, Revelation 5:12-14

Application: Who are you trusting for your sanctification? Who makes you holy? Is it you, trusting in your own careful observance of the *Torah*, or have you committed your life to Yeshua, the anointed King, High Priest and Messiah of Israel? Only He will never let you down or forsake you, for only He is "the Lamb of God who takes away the sin of the world" (John 1:29).

Sh'mini - Eighth

Vayikra / Leviticus 9:1 - 11:47

רִאשׁוֹן	Aliyah One	Vayikra/Leviticus 9:1 - 16
שֵׁנִי	Aliyah Two	Vayikra/Leviticus 9:17 - 23
שְׁלִישִׁי	Aliyah Three	Vayikra/Leviticus 9:24 - 10:11
רְבִיעִי	Aliyah Four	Vayikra/Leviticus 10:12 - 15
חֲמִשִׁי	Aliyah Five	Vayikra/Leviticus 10:16 - 20
שִׁשִּׁי	Aliyah Six	Vayikra/Leviticus 11:1 - 32
שְׁבִיעִי	Aliyah Seven	Vayikra/Leviticus 11:33 - 47

The text for Aliyah One in this *parasha* is out of sequence.

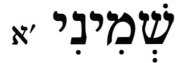

Sh'mini - Eighth - 1

Vayikra / Leviticus 9:1 - 16

Vayikra/Leviticus 11:47 Its purpose is to distinguish between the unclean and the clean

לְהַבְדִּיל בֵּין הַטָּמֵא וּבֵין הַטָּהֹר

ha'tahor ooveyn ha'tamey beyn l'hav'diyl

According to the Ramchal, the word טָמֵי (tamey) originates in the Hebrew root אָטַם (atam), which means 'to seal off' or 'to make impermeable', whereas טָהֹר (tahor) has the implication of 'transparent' or 'porous'. In modern Israel, the phrase *'cheder atum'* is only too familiar as the 'sealed room' that all new homes and apartments are required to have in case of poison gas attack.

But the *Torah* is using the words in a more spiritual sense: it is telling us that even in the everyday world of food, where there are things that are good and bad for us on a physical level, there is also an important spiritual lesson to be learned. Commenting on a few verses earlier in the chapter, the sages of the Talmud note that the word 'tamey' in verse 43 is deliberately misspelt without an aleph so that the word takes on the meaning 'stopped up' (*b.* Yoma 39*a*). Just as too much fat in our physical diet causes a thickening of the arteries and high cholesterol levels in the blood leading to angina and other serious heart conditions, so in the words of Rabbi Yishmael, "a transgression had the effect of stopping up a person's heart." Rashi comments that this means closing the heart to receiving wisdom.

Modern consumers have learnt to read the labels on the foods we buy in supermarkets. Many processed foods contain the warning "may contain traces of nuts" because of the life-threatening allergic reactions that some people may have to even the minutest amounts of nut in their food. Those with wheat or dairy intolerances may suffer hours of discomfort or misery from casually eating a dessert containing flour, cream or butter.

Some of the *kashrut* commands may seem arbitrary and even with the benefit of modern science and medicine we may not understand why they have been given. But just as eating food to which our physical bodies are sensitive will provoke an allergic reaction, whether we know the allergen is present or not, so the spiritual choices that we take affect our spiritual lives and relationships with God, whether we are fully aware of it or not. As the *Torah* says, "I call heaven and earth to witness against you today that I have presented you with life and death, the blessing and the curse. Therefore, choose life, so that you will live" (D'varim 30:19, CJB).

Further Study: 2 Corinthians 6:14-18; Matthew 5:19

Application: According to 1 John 1:6-7 there is a choice between walking in darkness and walking in the light. We need to be aware of these choices in our lives. Are you 'tamey' or 'tahor'?

שְׁמִינִי ב׳

Sh'mini - Eighth - 2

Vayikra / Leviticus 9:17 - 23

Vayikra/Leviticus 9:17 He brought near the grain offering ... and made it go up in smoke on the altar

וַיַּקְרֵב אֶת־הַמִּנְחָה ... וַיַּקְטֵר עַל־הַמִּזְבֵּחַ

ha'miz'beyakh al   vayak'teyr ... ha'minchah   et   vayak'reyv

This verse comes in the middle of Aharon's first day on duty as *Cohen Gadol*, High Priest. Nachmanides, the Ramban, discusses this verse in some detail, considering whether this grain offering is to be brought before, after or instead of the regular daily morning and evening offerings. The conclusion that he sees the Sages reaching is that this is a free-standing offering, offered each day by the High Priest, distinct from the grain offerings or drink offerings associated with any of the other offerings. Why is this important? Why does the Ramban devote a page and a half to reviewing this when the Sages have already discussed it in Torat Kohanim? The reason is because there is a prescribed form, ritual and pattern that Aharon and his sons have to follow - and this shows that they are following it. Aharon's two sons Nadab and Abihu died because they broke that pattern by bringing an offering that God had neither requested or authorised. The priests in general and the High Priest in particular were responsible for keeping to the precise form and ritual, for by it they not only demonstrate the constant nature of God but also God's unchanging attitude towards sin, the need for forgiveness and a right relationship with Him.

Rav Sha'ul wrote (albeit in a slightly different context) "God is not a God of confusion but of peace" (1 Corinthians 14:33, NASB). In other words, God doesn't have several conflicting sets of instructions, leaving us to try and guess which one is appropriate on the day. To borrow a modern saying: God doesn't speak out of both sides of His mouth! That is why when Yeshua says, "I AM the Way - and the Truth and the Life; no one comes to the Father except through Me" (John 14:6, CJB), we can be sure that He knew what He was talking about, and that the offer of salvation in Him is not only unique, but the only way to enter into a relationship with God.

Early in Mark's gospel we find the account of Yeshua healing a man afflicted with *tzara'at*. After He had healed him, "Yeshua sent him away with this stern warning: 'See to it that you tell no one; instead, as a testimony to the people, go and let the cohen examine you, and offer for your cleansing what Moshe commanded'" (Mark 1:43-44, CJB). Yeshua instructs the man, already healed, to submit to the standard procedure for re-admittance to the community once free of the *tzara'at* skin condition. Yeshua is acknowledging that there is a particular form, ritual, pattern to the proper order of things in the Kingdom of God, and teaching us to work that way ourselves by setting the example of doing it Himself. The key words in that narrative are "as a testimony to the people" - doing things God's way not only empowers our actions, but is the only way for an effective witness.

Further Study: 2 Samuel 6:6-11; Matthew 3:13-17

Application: Many people, including some who maintain that they are followers of Yeshua, live their lives as if they were following the old Frank Sinatra song, "I did it my way". Is that you, or do you always try to do things God's way? "In all your ways acknowledge Him and He will make your paths straight" (Proverbs 3:6, NASB).

שְׁמִינִי 'ג

Sh'mini - Eighth - 3

Vayikra / Leviticus 9:24 - 10:11

Vayikra/Leviticus 9:24 And fire went out from before the Lord and consumed on the altar the burnt offering

וַתֵּצֵא אֵשׁ מִלִּפְנֵי יהוה וַתֹּאכַל עַל־הַמִּזְבֵּחַ
hamizbeach al vatochal Adonai milifney eysh vateytzey

אֵת־הָעֹלָה
ha'olah et

The verb וַתֹּאכַל, here translated by the words "and consumed" is the *Qal* prefix 3fs form of the root אָכַל with a preceding *vav*-conversive construction. The root אָכַל occurs 795 times in the Hebrew Scriptures, most often with the meaning "to eat". Such a strong anthropomorphism makes some theologians and many believers quite uncomfortable: the idea of God actually eating sacrifices seeming both disgusting and a theological impossibility. Maimonedes' third principle says, "I believe with complete faith that the Creator, blessed be His name, is not physical and is not affected by physical phenomena" (Artscroll Siddur) and is echoed in the Yigdal prayer: "No form or shape has the incorporeal One" (Hertz Siddur). Yeshua Himself said, "God is spirit, and those who worship Him must worship in spirit and truth" (John 4:24, NASB).

Yet the fact remains that the text verse says, "fire came forth from the presence of Adonai, consuming the burnt offering and the fat on the altar. When all the people saw it, they shouted and fell on their faces" (CJB). Judaism very clearly stood apart from the surrounding cults and pagan religions where the people would manipulate or placate their all-too-human gods by bringing choice and costly offerings, as a bribe to ensure the god's favour or an attempt to win the god over to their point of view. The early chapters of Vayikra stipulate the types, quantities and frequencies of offerings to be brought for various situations and people, even distinguishing between the rich and the poor in prescribed ways so that access to God was available for all. The offering that Moshe and Aharon had just placed upon the altar was just such an offering - prescribed by God - and fire came down and all the people saw it and shouted.

Other examples of God breaking into the physical realm to accept an offering by fire include: "Then the angel of the Lord put out the end of the staff that was in his hand ... and fire sprang up from the rock and consumed the meat and unleavened bread" (Judges 6:21, NASB), "Elijah the prophet drew near ... then the fire of the Lord fell and consumed the burnt offering and the wood and the stones and the dust and licked up the water that was in the trench" (1 Kings 18:36,38, NASB), "Then David built an altar to the Lord there ... and He answered him with fire from heaven on the altar of burnt offering" (1 Chronicles 21:26, NASB). In all of these cases the fire serves as a clear sign of God's acceptance of the offering and a public endorsement of the people directly involved.

When Yeshua's disciples offered to call down fire from heaven as a sign of rebuke and displeasure on a Samaritan village who refused to accept Yeshua when He was travelling to Jerusalem, He in turn rebuked the disciples for making the suggestion saying, "The Son of Man did not come to destroy men's lives but to save them" (Luke 9:56, NASB). At least in part this may have been because a physical miracle would have compelled a response from the Samaritans and destroyed the possibility of a faith, free-will response which was what Yeshua was seeking.

Further Study: 2 Chronicles 7:1-3; Isaiah 29:13-14

Application: Do we often long for a physical sign or response from God to show that He has accepted our worship or is pleased with our actions? While natural enough, a dependence on miracles destroys our faith and "without faith it is impossible to please God" (Hebrews 11:6).

שְׁמִינִי ד׳

Sh'mini - Eighth - 4

Vayikra / Leviticus 10:12 - 15

Vayikra/Leviticus 10:12 Take the grain-offering, that which remains from the fire-offerings of Adonai

קְחוּ אֶת־הַמִּנְחָה הַנּוֹתֶרֶת מֵאִשֵּׁי יהוה

Adonai mey'ishey hanoteret haminkha   et   k'hu

At first glance, הַנּוֹתֶרֶת might look as if it were connected to the verb נָתַן, to give, for the fire-offerings were given to *HaShem*, but then the sense of the מִן־ preposition, "from, away from", elided on to the front of the following word, אִשֵּׁי, fire-offerings, would be entirely wrong. הַנּוֹתֶרֶת is the feminine singular - to agree with הַמִּנְחָה which is a feminine noun meaning literally "gift" but always taken in the context of the sacrificial system to mean a grain offering - *Niphal* participle of the root יָתַר, to be left or to remain; the participle having the sense of something that is left over or remains from a larger whole.

Aharon and his two remaining sons, Eleazar and Itamar - Nadab and Abihu having just died because they brought strange fire before the Lord (cf. 10:2) - are now commanded to eat the residual part - in fact, the majority - of the grain offering that was given to accompany the burnt offerings on the eighth day of the tabernacle's service, the first day that they are serving as fully inaugurated priests.

Rashi points out that this is the grain offering of Nahshon, the head of the tribe of Judah (cf. B'Midbar 7:12-17): "fine flour, mixed with oil". Because this is a public offering - Rashi's words are "a meal-offering of the hour" - that won't ever be brought again, since it was part of the ritual for setting up the tabernacle, Aharon and his sons have to eat the flour unleavened, or made into *matzah*, there by the altar in the holy place for "it is the holiest of holy things".

The grain offering served two purposes: firstly, it was eaten by the priests, as God's representatives, as a sign that God had accepted the offering as a whole; secondly, it was an important means of provision for the priests - a significant component of their diet! From this and the care with which the grain offering had to be handled and eaten - in the holy place and only by those who are ritually clean - we can learn several important lessons about the way that we bring offerings to the Lord. God intends that "those who proclaim the gospel [should] get their living from the gospel" (1 Corinthians 9:14, NASB). When Yeshua sent out the disciples through the towns and villages of the Galil, He told them, "Stay in that house, eating and drinking what they give you; for the labourer is worthy of his wages ... and whatever city you enter, and they receive you, eat what is set before you" (Luke 10:7-8, NASB). So the kingdom economy works that those who labour directly for God as teachers, evangelists, pastors, prophets and apostles (Ephesians 4:11) are supported by the community, according to their needs, as a part of the community's offerings to God. Similarly, many religious charities, working in education, outreach and among the poor, both at home and overseas, pay their workers suitable wages for their labour from the funds that are donated to those organisations as an essential part of delivering services. This too is right and proper, "for the Tanakh says, 'You are not to muzzle an ox when it is treading out the grain' (D'varim 25:4), in other words, 'the worker is worthy of his wages'" (1 Timothy 5:18, CJB).

We also learn the importance of stewardship over the resources that God provides. Those resources have been given by people to the Lord, sometimes at great personal cost, as an act of worship. It is therefore important that those who are responsible for administering and using those gifts do so in the fear of the Lord so that they should not be squandered or wasted. Larger organisations with staff, offices and overheads may be particularly challenged in this area, communicating the holiness of the offering to each and every employee without at the same time exploiting the workers; but all those who handle the kingdom economy have a duty of care to the Lord for the funds in their charge.

Further Study: 1 Corinthians 9:4-14; Luke 10:5-11

Application: As believers, we do have an obligation to give to the Lord and support those who work amongst us in the kingdom. For some, giving is by money, for others by prayer, for yet others practical help. Those who receive in turn give a proportion of their support to other kingdom activities. Whether you give or receive, do it for the Lord and His kingdom, exercising due diligence to serve Him well.

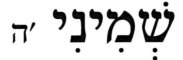

Sh'mini - Eighth - 5

Vayikra / Leviticus 10:16 - 20

Vayikra/Leviticus 10:16 And Moshe specifically enquired about the goat of the sin offering

וְאֵת | שְׂעִיר הַחַטָּאת דָּרֹשׁ דָּרַשׁ מֹשֶׁה

Moshe darash darosh ha'khatat s'iyr v'eyt

Rashi tells us that three goats were offered on that day: the one for the inaugural offering (Vayikra 9:1-4); one that was part of the offering of "Nahshon the son of Amminadav,of the tribe of Judah" (B'Midbar 7:13 NASB), who was the first of the tribal leaders to bring identical offerings in the first twelve days of the tabernacle's operation; and, since we know that this was the first day of the month of Nissan (B'Midbar 9:1, Shemot 40:17), there was also, "one male goat for a sin offering to the Lord" (B'Midbar 28:15, NASB) for the *Rosh Chodesh* offerings. Which one was Moshe asking about? It must be the sin offering for the people (Vayikra 9:3), for the others are not mentioned explicitly in the text; this is the goat of the sin offering.

Moshe wants to know what has happened to the flesh of the goat; by regulation it should have been eaten by the priests in the holy place - has this happened, he wants to know; has everything been done properly? In fact, it had been burnt, the fall-back position for most holy things, because of Aharon's distress - the only evidence we have of it - over the death of his two sons Nadab and Abihu. The principle of the proper disposition of most holy things is taken up in the Mishnah, where the rabbis debate whether the laws of sacrilege or the laws of remnant, refuse and uncleanness should apply to the most holy things that have been handled incorrectly. Provided that the blood has been tossed upon the altar, then the sacrifice is considered valid and the atonement takes place, even if the flesh has not been eaten in the proper place or time, but the flesh must then be burnt upon the altar as well as the fat. Rabbi Eliezer and Rabbi Akiva have an exchange (*m.* Meilah 1:2-3) about an animal that manages to escape from the sanctuary after it has been dedicated but before it can be sacrificed, or whose flesh was taken out of the sanctuary inadvertently after slaughter but before the blood had been tossed upon the altar - a discussion that remained open until the Talmud several hundred years later and even then, in some opinions, wasn't fully resolved.

Why was this so important? Why was Moshe so exercised that the text uses two adjacent forms of the same verb, "to enquire about, he enquired", a construction usually translated using the words 'certainly' or 'surely' to emphasis the action. The root, דָּרַשׁ, has the meanings: to seek or to search for, to seek after, to enquire, to ask for or demand; and is commonly encountered in the Hebrew word used to describe such pieces of commentary as this. Moshe was not content simply to ask the question and receive a casual reply from someone who happened to have been there and might have seen what happened, he wanted to know exactly what had occurred so he went directly to the people involved - on this occasion Aharon and his sons - to find out for himself, because he was concerned that on the very first day that the tabernacle was officially "open for business" everything should be done in accordance with God's instructions.

On one of the occasions that Rav Sha'ul arrived in Ephesus, he found a few *talmidim*. He asked them, "'Did you receive the Ruach HaKodesh when you came to trust?' 'No,' they said to him, 'we have never even heard that there is such a thing as the Ruach HaKodesh'" (Acts 19:1-2, CJB). These disciples knew about sin and repentance and were trying to follow God; they had been baptised in line with John the Baptiser's ministry, but had not heard the full gospel message of Yeshua, the One of whom John spoke. Sha'ul explained to them about Yeshua and they believed in Him, "and when Sha'ul placed his hands on them, the Ruach HaKodesh came upon them; so that they were speaking in tongues and prophesying" (v. 6, CJB). Although these disciples were intent on serving God, they only had half the picture and could not move forward without hearing the rest of the story; once they did, they entered fully into the kingdom. How important it was for them to know and understand fully what God was saying so that they could respond and enter into the truth.

A while earlier, on Rav Sha'ul's first journey into Greece, he and Silas entered the town of Berea; "As soon as they arrived, they went to the synagogue. Now the people here ... eagerly welcomed the message, checking the Tanakh every day to see if the things Sha'ul was saying were true. Many of them came to trust" (Acts 17:10-12, CJB). The men of Berea wanted to hear the message that Sha'ul brought and they liked what they heard, but they needed to be sure that it was the truth, so they spent time to checking that all the references were correct, and that what Sha'ul said was consistent with what God had said before. Was Rav Sha'ul irritated that they didn't just believe him? On the contrary, the text praises the noble character of the Bereans for taking that time and trouble so that when they committed themselves to faith in Yeshua it would be whole-hearted, in full possession of the facts; they would be able to defend their position and not be shaken by those who disagreed with them. Like Moshe, they needed to know the facts, so they went to the source and checked up for themselves.

Luke begins his gospel account with an important statement: "since I have carefully investigated these things from the beginning, it seemed good to me that I should write you an accurate and ordered narrative, so that you might know how well-founded are the things about which you have been taught" (Luke 1:3-4, CJB). Luke knew how important it was that Theophilus should have a reliable reference for checking the facts of his faith in Yeshua. God wants us all to be well informed and certain about the facts of our faith. Like Moshe, He wants us to ask hard questions of the right people - Himself - and find satisfactory answers through the pages of the Bible, guided by the Holy Spirit and sound teachers who will explain the texts to us and encourage us in our faith.

Further Study: 2 Timothy 3:14-15; 1 Peter 1:10-12

Application: Are you asking the questions? Are you asking the right person? Now is the time to engage with God and make sure that you understand what He requires of you and what He is offering you! Stand firm in your relationship with God and make the time to know the facts straight from the One who knows!

שְׁמִינִי 'ו

Sh'mini - Eighth - 6

Vayikra / Leviticus 11:1 - 32

Vayikra/Leviticus 11:2 These are the living things that you shall eat from all the animals that are on the earth

זֹאת הַחַיָּה אֲשֶׁר תֹּאכְלוּ מִכָּל־הַבְּהֵמָה אֲשֶׁר
asher habheymah mikol tochlu asher hakhayah zot

עַל־הָאָרֶץ:
ha'aretz al

On the basis of the words immediately preceding our text, דַּבְּרוּ אֶל־בְּנֵי יִשְׂרָאֵל - "Speak to the children of Israel", Rashi claims that the following dietary regulations apply to all the Israelites and so to all Jews today. Moshe and Aharon were told to speak to all the people, not just Aharon and his sons, or to the elders of Israel. The Ramban, on the other hand, while agreeing that "these sections apply to both Israelites and the priests" qualifies that by adding "but their subject-matter affects mostly the priests, for they must always guard themselves from touching impure objects, since they have to come into the Sanctuary". The Ramban is saying that because they serve God and come into His presence in the tabernacle, the priests have to be especially careful about their status of purity otherwise they may become disqualified from being able to serve. Moreover, as the priests were also charged with the responsibility of teaching the Israelites "how to distinguish the sacred from the profane and the unclean from the clean" (Vayikra 10:10), it was important that they understand and implement these requirements for themselves.

Targum Onkelos translates the words הַחַיָּה - here literally, the living thing or the life, singular - and הַבְּהֵמָה - again, literally, the animal, singular - with חֵיְתָא and בְּעִרָא. While the two words are normally used to compare wild animals and domestic animals, the Bechor Schor comments that in this context, this means healthy animals. He is supported by the Ba'al HaTurim who states that "An animal that is healthy", meaning one that is

59

not only living but capable of remaining alive, "you may eat, but an animal that is not healthy, you may not eat." Notice that the question of *kosher* or non-*kosher* animals is not in view in these comments; it is assumed that any animal being considered for eating is already *kosher* according to its genus (species) and method of slaughtering - all that is here being discussed is whether the animal is sick or healthy.

Collecting together the views of several well and lesser known commentators, Nechama Leibowitz explores the reasons for the dietary laws being given to Israel. Modern scholars, pointing to the fact that dietary laws were common in ancient cultures, try to find a connection between various animals and foods, and good and evil spiritual forces who were imagined to be fighting between themselves. Leibowitz comments, "there is nothing intrinsically unclean, evil or demonic in living creatures. Thus in Genesis all living creatures are the work of God, the sole Creator who fashioned from the ground 'all the beasts of the earth and fowl of the heaven' (B'resheet 9:2). They are therefore merely unclean to you - forbidden as food to you." Maimonides offers a medical basis for the dietary laws: "The principle reason why the *Torah* forbids swine's flesh is to be found in the circumstances that its habits and its food are very dirty and loathsome" (Guide for the Perplexed 3,48), but this is rejected by many commentators such as the Akedat Yitzkhak: "We ought to bear in mind that the dietary laws are not, as some have asserted, motivated by therapeutic considerations, God forbid! Were that so, the *Torah* would be reduced to the level of a minor medical treatise." The Sforno comments that "God thus forbade the foods that defile the soul morally and intellectually", trying to make the reason for the restrictions apply at a spiritual rather than a physical level. Others see the dietary laws as part of the way of distinguishing Israel from the nations, that they might be a set apart and holy people to the Lord: "Every Jew must set himself apart by keeping laws and principles that differ from those of the pagan nations. He must not imitate them, but cleave to the God of his forefathers." (S. D. Luzzatto). Leibowitz, however, both dismisses and sums up these opinions by saying, "the more we rationalise such prohibitions as intrinsically noxious to body or soul, the farther we drift from their actual basis" and closes with a quote from Sifra, Kedoshim 128: "Rabbi Elazar ben Azarya says: One should not say: I dislike wearing *sha'atnez*, or eating pork; rather one should say, I crave these but what can I do - my Father in Heaven has prohibited these!"

With that as a background, Yeshua called the people together and said to them, "There is nothing outside a person which, by going into him, can make him unclean. Rather, it is the things that come out of a person which make a person unclean." (Mark 7:15, CJB). The disciples were puzzled; they asked Him what He was talking about. "Don't you see that nothing going into a person from outside can make him unclean? For it doesn't go into his heart but into his stomach, and it passes out into the latrine. (Thus he declared all foods ritually clean)" (vv. 18-19, CJB). Does this mean that Yeshua is voiding the dietary laws? Generations of Christian commentators have similarly been confused about what Yeshua was saying because they have ignored the context in which Yeshua was speaking and His immediate audience. When this originally spoken, it was said to an exclusively Jewish audience and following a debate with the Pharisees and *Torah*-teachers about the observance of the Traditions of the Elders, in particular the requirement to wash the hands before eating. This sets the debate clearly in the context of an "internal" Jewish debate about the dietary laws - which, like the comments of the Ba'al HaTurim above take certain things for granted; in particular, it defined the word 'food' as meaning something that apart from the matter immediately being discussed is otherwise completely *kosher*. Yeshua - and any Jew of His time - did not consider pig meat as food. The key word to notice in Yeshua's statement is "ritually" - Yeshua is saying that anything that is food (for the people concerned) is ritually clean and that its status as *kosher* is not dependent on the person eating it or the ritual surrounding the eating. Eating something that you know to be unclean, or that has been involved in harmful spiritual practices - such as Rav Sha'ul is later going to explain when talking about food that has been offered to idols (Romans 14 and 2 Corinthians 6) - or in the wrong way, is a human choice that makes the eater unclean, regardless of the food itself. After listing unacceptable forms of behaviour, Yeshua makes it clear what He is talking about: "All these wicked things come from within, and they make a person unclean" (v. 23, CJB).

Physically eating the food that is "allowed" for you is a matter of simple obedience to the commands that God has given you. If you are Jewish then pork and shellfish are not defined as 'food' for you and eating them is, while probably not directly harmful to your physical health, disobedience; if you are Gentile then this does not apply to you, although it is important to make sure that pork is properly cooked to ensure that the bacteria and parasites present in the meat are killed before you eat it.

The same rules apply to our spiritual diet. What do we take into our spirits, our minds, by what we read, listen to and watch? How do we allow "the prince of the power of the air" (Ephesians 2:2, NASB) to feed our souls? Many believers feel that this is a matter of personal judgement and freedom; that they are free to choose what they read and watch, what they take into their minds. In one sense that is true, since God has given us all freedom of choice, but, just as with physical food, Rav Sha'ul explains: "All things are lawful, but not all things are profitable. All things are lawful, but not all things edify" (1 Corinthians 10:23, NASB). Not everything is profitable for our minds and not everything builds up our souls in a manner that is helpful and healthy according to kingdom standards. Sha'ul defines the boundary for us: "In conclusion, brothers, focus your thoughts on what is true, noble, righteous, pure, lovable or admirable, on some virtue or on something praiseworthy. Keep doing what you have learned and received from me, what you have heard and seen me doing; then the God who gives shalom will be with you" (Philippians 4:8-9, CJB). In order to know God's peace, in order not get get spiritual indigestion or parasites, we need to exclude anything from our spiritual diet that falls outside these limits. However much we might protest, it is a simple matter of obedience. To quote Rabbi Elazar: what can I do - my Father in Heaven has prohibited these!

Further Study: Psalm 34:5; 2 Peter 3:13-14

Application: Are you sure that you only read and watch things that Yeshua would approve and be happy to sit and watch with you? If not, why not ask Him to show you where your reading or viewing material falls outside the limits He has set for you? He wants us all to clean up our act and be spiritually clean and healthy before Him so that we may be a part of the pure, radiant and spotless bride.

שְׁמִינִי 'ז

Sh'mini - Eighth - 7

Vayikra / Leviticus 11:33 - 47

Vayikra/Leviticus 11:33 And any earthenware vessel into which any of them fall, everything that is in it will become unclean

וְכָל־כְּלִי־חֶרֶשׂ אֲשֶׁר־יִפֹּל מֵהֶם אֶל־תּוֹכוֹ כֹּל
kol   tocho el meyhem yipol asher kheres k'liy v'chol

אֲשֶׁר בְּתוֹכוֹ יִטְמָא
yitma b'tocho asher

This is one of those verses that generates significant discussion between the early sages; nearly a whole page of the Talmud is given over to this subject before the discussion widens to consider wooden and metal vessels, before, during and after manufacture. The word תָּוֶךְ, present here as תּוֹכוֹ and בְּתוֹכוֹ, is responsible for the debate. Meaning simply "the middle, midst", it is almost always used with a preposition - in, from, to - and usually in either construct or possessive form: "in their midst", "from the midst of ...". The "them" in the verse refers to unclean creeping things, such as frogs and lizards, whose bodies may fall into containers.

The controversy here centres around the unusual proposition that an earthenware vessel - which is, because of its physical nature, slightly porous - and its contents, become unclean from the inside rather than the outside. "Our Rabbis taught: It is written: And every earthen vessel into which any of them falls, that is to say, even though it does not actually touch the vessel" (*b.* Chullin 24*b*). R. Ada ben Ahabah asked Raba why, if it can be made unclean from the inside, it can't also be made unclean from the outside and he replies by making a connection to the verse "And every open vessel, which has no covering tied down on it, shall be unclean" (B'Midbar 19:15, NASB), that since only uncovered vessels become unclean, it must be that the uncleanness comes only from the inside and not from the outside. Expanding the argument to the air-space inside the vessel, Abravanel comments, "even if [the unclean dead body] is hanging in the air and does not actually touch the vessel, everything inside the vessel is unclean". This means not only that the vessel itself becomes unclean, but all of its contents - even if they are not touching the vessel - also become unclean.

Of course, Yeshua would have been well aware of these issues, as earthenware pots were frequently used for storage and cooking in those days. Doubtless, He had it in mind when He was debating with the Pharisees: "Woe to you, scribes and Pharisees, hypocrites! For you clean the outside of the cup and of the dish, but inside they are full of robbery and self-indulgence. You blind Pharisee, first clean the inside of the cup and of the dish, so that the outside of it may become clean also" (Matthew 23:25-26, NASB). Yeshua was using the inside/outside impurity issue as a way to talk about the Pharisees' behaviour and conduct; they seemed clean and respectable on the outside, but were morally corrupt on the inside. In Luke's account of the debate, Yeshua goes a step further: "Now you Pharisees clean the outside of the cup and of the platter; but inside of you, you are full of robbery and wickedness. You foolish ones, did not He who made the outside make the inside also? But give that which is within as charity, and then all things are clean for you" (Luke 11:39-41, NASB). If the Pharisees were to give their ill-gotten wealth or status away as charity - the Hebrew word צְדָקָה is here used as a word play, as it can mean both charitable donations or works and righteousness - then their "inside space" would be clean, so all of them would be clean from the inside out.

The third place in which Yeshua covers this ground is in a different context. Mark chapter seven is often misused by people to try and show that Yeshua abrogated the *kosher* dietary laws for Jewish people, releasing them from the obligation to eat only *kosher* food as specified in the *Torah*. Without visiting that particular argument here[5], look at the way Yeshua uses the concept. Having called the multitude around Him to listen, He tells them, "Listen to Me, all of you, and understand: there is nothing outside the man which going into him can defile him; but the things which proceed out of the man are what defile the man" (Mark 7:14-15, NASB). Man is like an earthenware vessel and cannot be made impure from the outside; it is the "air space" inside a man that causes impurity. The *talmidim* didn't understand the connection that He was making, so He then outlines it again in more explicit terms for them: "Do you not understand that whatever goes into the man from outside cannot defile him; because it does not go into his heart, but into his stomach, and is eliminated?" (vv. 18-19, NASB). The real centre of a man's personality, his soul, what makes him human, the divine spark, is not his stomach but his heart; food simply goes through the digestive system. A Jew who innocently eats non-*kosher* food has not become impure simply because of food that he has eaten in good faith; one who chooses to eat non-*kosher* food or fails to ask the appropriate questions

---

5. See the previous commentary, *Shemini* 6 for that discussion

or make the necessary checks has become impure not because of the food, but because his heart either took a decision to disobey God's instructions or couldn't be bothered to obey them.

So Yeshua goes on: "That which proceeds out of the man, that is what defiles the man. For from within, out of the heart of men, proceed the evil thoughts, fornications, thefts, murders, adulteries, deeds of coveting and wickedness, as well as deceit, sensuality, envy, slander, pride and foolishness. All these evil things proceed from within and defile the man" (Mark 7:20-23, NASB). These are not food substances, simply passing through the alimentary canal before elimination, these are habits, thoughts and practices which are stored in the heart of the unregenerate man. Sadly, they are also often stored in the heart of those who claim to be believers but are reluctant to give up their secret sins. Simply cleaning up the outside of our lives, while harbouring sin within, makes us just like the Pharisees who have cleaned the outside of the cup so that all those who see them think that they have got their act together, but in truth "are like whitewashed tombs which on the outside appear beautiful, but inside they are full of dead men's bones and all uncleanness" (Matthew 23:27, NASB).

Of course all of us have moments of weakness, when we think thoughts that are not loving and charitable, when we absent-mindedly allow images and words that are not "true, honorable, right, pure, lovely, of good repute, of excellence and worthy of praise" (Philippians 4:8, my paraphrase) into our hearts. But these are easily dealt with; the moment you realise what you are doing, confess it to the Lord, kick the thoughts out and seek His forgiveness and cleansing - "If we confess our sins, He is faithful and righteous to forgive us our sins and to cleanse us from all unrighteousness" (1 John 1:9, NASB). Get up off the floor and move on, resolving not to do that again.

More difficult to handle are those acts of deliberate indulgence, when we choose to flirt with the temptations that the enemy has dangled in our path, when we play with the ideas - not, perhaps, intending to actually do anything about them - until, without us having really been aware of exactly how it has happened, they become a part of us and we find ourselves doing or saying something out of that sin. Then Yeshua's words are true of us: the impurity proceeds from within and defiles us. Our "air space", our internal selves, has been corrupted by the presence of the impurity. But Yeshua's remedy for the Pharisees still applies: "first clean the inside of the cup and of the dish" (Matthew 23:26, NASB), "surrender the things inside for the sake of righteousness and then you will be clean from the inside out" (Luke 11:41, my paraphrase). We have to acknowledge that we have engaged in deliberate sin and repent, agreeing with God's word that "like sheep, we have gone astray, each of us has turned to our own way" (Isaiah 53:6), then surrender the thoughts and activities to Him, being prepared to completely abandon them and give them up in order to be righteous and acceptable before Him.

Recovery is always possible, although it may need time and healing to restore someone from significant sin.

This is not worm theology. Earthenware vessels we may be, fragile, liable to cracking and susceptible to impurity, but we are nevertheless chosen and precious to God, the vehicles in which He has chosen to display His grace and riches for all the world to see. "But we have this treasure in earthen vessels, that the surpassing greatness of the power may be of God and not from ourselves; we are afflicted in every way, but not crushed; perplexed, but not despairing; persecuted, but not forsaken; struck down, but not destroyed" (2 Corinthians 4:7-9, NASB).

Further Study: Colossians 2:16; Titus 1:15

Application: Do you struggle on an almost daily basis to keep the impurity out of your "inner space"? The tight-fitting lid of the Holy Spirit will protect you, if you ask Him. Then "the peace of God, which surpasses all understanding, will guard your hearts and your minds in Messiah Yeshua" (Philippians 4:7).

תַזְרִיעַ/מְצֹרָה

Tazriya/Metzorah - She will conceive/One with tzara'at

Vayikra / Leviticus 12:1 - 15:33

- in leap years, the two *parashiyot* are read separately; in regular years, they are read together -

רִאשׁוֹן	Aliyah One	Vayikra/Leviticus 12:1 - 13:23
שְׁלִישִׁי	Aliyah Three	Vayikra/Leviticus 13:38 - 54
רְבִיעִי	Aliyah Four	Vayikra/Leviticus 13:55 - 14:20
שִׁשִּׁי	Aliyah Six	Vayikra/Leviticus 14:33 - 15:15
שְׁבִיעִי	Aliyah Seven	Vayikra/Leviticus 15:16 - 33

תַזְרִיעַ - Vayikra/Leviticus 12:1 - 13:59

| שֵׁנִי | Aliyah Two | Vayikra/Leviticus 13:6 - 17 |
| חֲמִשִׁי | Aliyah Five | Vayikra/Leviticus 13:29 - 37 |

מְצֹרָע - Vayikra/Leviticus 14:1 - 15:33

| שֵׁנִי | Aliyah Two | Vayikra/Leviticus 14:13 - 20 |
| חֲמִשִׁי | Aliyah Five | Vayikra/Leviticus 14:54 - 15:15 |

תַזְרִיַ/מְצֹרָה 'א

Tazriya/Metzorah - She will conceive/One with tzara'at - 1

(In a leap year this could be read as Tazria 1)

Vayikra / Leviticus 12:1 - 13:23

Vayikra/Leviticus 12:2 "When a woman conceives and gives birth to a male ..."

אִשָּׁה כִּי תַזְרִיעַ וְיָלְדָה זָכָר

zachar v'yaldah taz'riya kiy ishah

The Rabbis discuss this phrase at some length in the *Midrash*. Rabbi Levi said, "Human beings entrust to Him a drop of fluid in privacy, and the Holy One, blessed be He, openly returns to them completed and perfected human beings. Is this not a matter for praise?" (Vayikra Rabbah 14.2). In other words, Rabbi Levi is acknowledging that control over the creation of life is a matter for God and not for the husband and wife who happen to engage in sexual relations. Just as the gender of a child is beyond the control of man, so is the creation of the life itself. Some couples remain childless, others have children early or late but not both, while others seem to produce offspring regularly throughout the normal child-bearing years.

Once conceived, Rabbi Abba bar Kahana comments that, "the embryo has its own abode in the mother's womb, but the Holy One, blessed be He, guards it so that it shall not fall out and die. This then is the meaning of 'You granted me life and grace, Your careful attention preserved my spirit' (Job 10:12, CJB)" (Vayikra Rabbah 14.3). Again, the Rabbis' attention is drawn to God's provenance in guarding and protecting the unborn child during pregnancy. The prophet Isaiah testifies to the end of the process: "'Shall I bring to the point of birth, and not give delivery?', says the Lord. 'Or shall I who gives delivery shut the womb?' says your God" (Isaiah 66:9, NASB).

God has plans and purposes, not only for each of us as individuals (Jeremiah 29:11 ff.) but for His people as a whole. Just as a pregnancy has a certain length, from conception to birth, over which man has little natural control, so events happen in the spiritual realm according to God's calendar rather than that of men. Someone has said that the moment of power is at the intersection of man's preparation and God's timing. Often, it is simply a matter of waiting and allowing God's plans to work through our obedience and patience.

When we count the *Omer* from *Pesach* to *Shavuot*, we need to remember Yeshua's instructions to His disciples, "you shall be baptised with the Ruach HaKodesh not many days from now" (Acts 1:5, NASB) as He was taken from them into heaven. *Shavuot* will come, as it always does, one day after the seventh sabbath, fifty days from the start of the count. Our people met with *Adonai* on Mt. Sinai to receive the *Torah* in smoke, fire and the sound of the *shofar* (Shemot 19:18ff), 50 days after leaving Egypt. The *Ruach HaKodesh* was poured out on the same day thousands of years later in wind and fire (Acts 2:1 ff.). It was just a matter of waiting.

Further Study: Psalm 40:1-3; Acts 1:6-8

Application: All of our lives go through cycles, up times and down times. Our strength comes from knowing that God is constant and never changes. He is not fickle or capricious as man can be - we may wobble but He is always faithful and true.

תַזְרִיעַ 'ב

Tazriya - She will conceive - 2

(In an ordinary year this could be read as Tazria/Metzorah 1)

Vayikra / Leviticus 13:6 - 17

Vayikra/Leviticus 13:6 And the priest shall see him on the seventh day a second time

וְרָאָה הַכֹּהֵן אֹתוֹ בַּיּוֹם הַשְּׁבִיעִי שֵׁנִית

sheyniyt hashviyiy bayom   oto   hakoheyn v'ra'ah

The word שֵׁנִית (an adjective, used here in feminine form as an adverb, meaning 'a second time' or 'again') is at first glance misleading because this is actually the third time that the *cohen* will have seen the person who may be afflicted with *tzara'at*. The first time he would have placed the sufferer in isolation for seven days; the second time was at the end of that first seven-day period, when a second week in isolation would be prescribed if necessary. The text describes the third inspection at the end of the second block of seven days. Only if at this third inspection, after two waiting periods for the condition to clear, *tzara'at* is still present is the person declared unclean.

John Ortberg, in his book 'Love Beyond Reason', has a chapter entitled "The Lord of the Second Chance", in which he educates the non-golf-playing readers about the wonders of a 'mulligan': if your shot shies crazily off the course and becomes completely unplayable, then you simply disregard it, you don't write it down - as if it had never existed - you 'take a mulligan'. Do you remember Yeshua doing the same thing?

In John 21 we find the passage where Yeshua rehabilitates Peter over breakfast. But see how the narrative paints in the 'second chance' motif. After the *talmidim* have been out all night fishing and caught nothing, Yeshua "said to them, 'You don't have any fish, do you?' 'No,' they answered Him. He said to them, 'Throw in your net to starboard and you will catch some.' So they threw in their net, and there were so many in it that they couldn't haul it aboard" (v. 5-6, CJB). Doesn't that remind you of Luke 5:1-11 when Yeshua first called Peter? But it goes on: "when they got out upon the land, they saw a charcoal fire already laid" (v. 9, NASB), because a few chapters earlier, Peter had stood warming himself by a charcoal fire in the courtyard of the *Cohen Gadol* when he denied Yeshua for the first time (John 18:18). That's why when "Yeshua said to them, 'Come and have breakfast.' None of the talmidim dared to ask Him, 'Who are you?' They knew it was the Lord" (21:12, CJB). And then Yeshua restored Peter by asking him three times to confirm that he loved Him; three times to reverse the three denials.

God always wants to give us a second chance if we will take it from Him - the choice is ours. In one of the great passages from the Tanakh, God says: "'Come now, let us reason together,' says the Lord; 'though your sins are like scarlet, they shall be white as snow; though they are like crimson, they shall become like wool'" (Isaiah 1:18, ESV).

Further Study: Micah 6:2-8; Revelation 7:13-17

Application: Have you blown it recently? Do you need a second chance? God is just waiting to help you do precisely that. Ask Him if you can take a mulligan and get it off your chest.

תַּזְרִיעַ

Tazriya - She will conceive - 5

(In an ordinary year this could be read as Tazria/Metzorah 2)

Vayikra / Leviticus 13:29 - 37

Vayikra/Leviticus 13:30 And the priest shall see the affliction

וְרָאָה הַכֹּהֵן אֶת־הַנֶּגַע

hanega   et   hacoheyn   v'ra'a

This text is in the context of "a man or a woman in whom there will be an affliction, on the scalp or in the beard" (13:29, Artscroll). As with other instances of *tzara'at*, the priest is called upon to decide whether this is indeed *tzara'at* or simply a blemish or infection of another kind. As usual, the cohen is provided with a detailed description of by which to make his assessment: "deeper than the skin, and there is thin yellow hair in it" (v. 30, NASB). If the description matches, then the *cohen* is to pronounce the person unclean - it is *tzara'at*. Then follow one or two weeks of isolation to see how the affliction progresses, at the end of which other inspections may result in in the person being declared clean once more, or the unclean state continuing. Notice, however, that the *cohen* is not a doctor: he looks but does not cure, he offers no prescription or treatment other than the formal isolation that the *Torah* itself prescribes; his role is simply to arbitrate on the basis of the description or template of the condition the *Torah* provides and the condition of the person - then to issue a formal pronouncement of status. This is why after healing the leper - more accurately, the person with *tzara'at* - Yeshua sends him to the priest: to receive the formal status of 'clean', to bring the appropriate sacrifice and be accepted back into society; "Go, show yourself to the priest, and present the offering that Moshe commanded, for a testimony to them" (Matthew 8:4, CJB).

Yeshua Himself teaches that we too are not only capable of making, but are required to make, this kind of determination. "Beware of false prophets! They come to you wearing sheep's clothing, but underneath they are hungry wolves! You will recognise them by their fruit" (Matthew 7:15-16, CJB). We have an obligation, for ourselves and for those who depend on our opinion or discernment, to assess others with whom we come into contact to ensure that they are not in a position to cause harm or damage. Here, as for the *cohen* in the sequence from the *Torah*, Yeshua provides a template to make the assessment that details the criteria to be used: "Can people pick grapes from thorn bushes, or figs from thistles? Likewise every healthy tree produces good fruit, but a poor tree produces bad fruit. A healthy tree cannot produce bad fruit, or a poor tree good fruit" (vv. 16-18, CJB). All sorts of other criteria that we might want to use - such as income, parentage, colour, speech, clothing - are conspicuously absent; Yeshua is interested in the fruit that is being produced in a person's life, the qualities they display - almost subconsciously - as they go about their normal business and living rather than set-piece performances put on for the benefit of others. Rav Sha'ul lists the fruit that God desires: "the fruit of the Spirit is love, joy, peace, patience, kindness, goodness, faithfulness, humility, self-control" (Galatians 5:22-23, CJB); it is these that we should expect to see being manifest in a good tree in the Kingdom of God. The rabbis agree: "Merit has a capital value and also bears fruit [interest], as it is stated, 'Say ye of the righteous, that it shall go well with him, for they shall eat the fruit of their doings' (Isaiah 3:10)" (Avot d'Rabbi Natan).

Yeshua closes by repeating his first injunction: "So you will recognise them by their fruit" (Matthew 7:20, CJB), and the words of the translation are chosen with care, for recognition is not the same as judgement. Throughout Yeshua's words and in the sequence from the *Torah*, no mention is made of judgement. The *cohen* pronounces the current status of the affliction or blemish; he does not make any comment as to how it got there, what behaviour, actions or attitudes might have contributed to it, or remedial action that implies a judgement of the person or their values. Likewise, Yeshua does not allow us to judge those around us; on the contrary, only a few verses earlier He explicitly says, "Don't judge, so that you won't be judged" (7:1, CJB). Judgement is only available for those who are in an appropriate authority structure and area of responsibility: a doctor makes a judgement (diagnosis) about illness; a policeman makes a judgement (ticket/citation) about traffic violations; a chef makes a judgement (menu) about food and recipes - and all of them issue appropriate instructions to correct, remedy or pay for problems! Except for those in positions of spiritual authority - pastors of churches/congregations, husbands/fathers of families, counsellors of clients - who are given or granted a limited authority, we are none of us in a position to judge our fellows on moral or religious grounds. More, none of us at all ever have the right to judge another human being's worth or value; that belongs to God alone. If we step into that position, either deliberately or inadvertently, then we develop attitudes, build walls and make meaningful relationships with other people impossible.

Further Study: D'varim 19:15-21; 1 Timothy 5:19-20

Application: How do you assess people and situations? Do you use your own standards or are you careful only to see God's standards and templates? Remember that while we have a responsibility to exercise discernment, we must not enter into judgement but always try to leave the channels of communication open.

תַזְרִיעַ/מְצֹרָה 'ג

Tazriya/Metzorah - She will conceive/One with tzara'at - 3

(In a leap year this could be read as Tazria 6)

Vayikra / Leviticus 13:38 - 54

Vayikra/Leviticus 13:38 If there is, in the skin of their flesh, a shining scurf, white

כִּי־יִהְיֶה בְעוֹר־בְּשָׂרָם בֶּהָרֹת בֶּהָרֹת לְבָנֹת:

l'vanot   beharot   beharot   b'saram   v'or   yih'yeh kiy

Davidson analyses בֶּהָרֹת as a feminine plural noun from an unused root בָּהַר, which in Arabic means "to shine"; he gives the meaning as "a shining, whitish scurf, sinking in the skin and having white hair". Rashi, somewhat laconically, simply provides a one-word note: spots. The word is repeated both for emphasis and to indicate that there are likely to be several patches or areas, rather than just a single point. Whatever its precise physiological appearance, this is one of the several and somewhat diverse physical manifestations of *tzara'at*, a word for which translators and commentators over the centuries have struggled to convey an accurate meaning. Part of the problem is that it affects people, buildings and clothing, which a physical disease or infestation does not do; its appearance does not match leprosy or any of the known skin diseases or infections known to medicine, and the sheer variety of its forms makes it difficult to identify from a scientific point of view.

Maimonedes, in his commentary on the Mishnah, *Nega'im* 12:5, states: "Our Sages have said that *tzara'at* comes as a punishment for the evil tongue, for its owner is isolated and can no longer harm people with his loose talk." Martin Buber comments: "According to the conception of *Torah*, *tzara'at* is an impurity which afflicts the affected body or object, and impurity implies the marring of the relationship between God and man". So *tzara'at* can be seen as a spiritual or supernatural reflection of sin or a relationship breakdown between man and *HaShem*; a physical sign given by

God in increasing levels of severity (person, clothing, house) to make somebody wake up and focus their attention on putting things right - and in all cases, it requires significant isolation or separation so that the afflicted person or items become untouchable, removed from normal society.

It was in that context that we read the gospel accounts of Yeshua's encounters with those whom society defined as excluded and untouchable. "A man afflicted with tzara'at came, kneeled down in front of Him and said, 'Sir, if You are willing, You can make me clean.' Yeshua reached out His hand, touched him and said, 'I am willing! Be cleansed!' And at once he was cleansed from his tzara'at" (Matthew 8:2-3, CJB). The man knew that he was untouchable, because anyone who touched him would themselves become ritually unclean, so he simply asks to be made clean. Yeshua, on the other hand, knows that the man needs contact in more ways than just verbal in order to be healed, so He breaks through the ritual barrier and touches the man and speaks the words of healing. The man is healed in response to the touch and the words - God broke through into his life!

Further Study: 2 Kings 5:9-14; Psalm 144:5-7; Matthew 14:35-36

Application: Are there people in your life that you treat as 'untouchable'? Relationships that have broken down to nothing more than polite but sterile existence? Now is the time to break through that barrier and - prompted and empowered by the *Ruach HaKodesh* - touch, speak words of comfort and faith, and see God's healing take place.

תַזְרִי/מְצֹרָה ד'

Tazriya/Metzorah - She will conceive/One with tzara'at - 4

(In a leap yesr this could be read as Tazria 7)

Vayikra / Leviticus 13:55 - 14:20

Vayikra/Leviticus 13:55 And the priest will look, after washing the affliction, and behold - the affliction has not changed its colour

וְרָאָה הַכֹּהֵן אַחֲרֵי | הֻכַּבֵּס אֶת־הַנֶּגַע וְהִנֵּה

v'hiney hanega' et hukabeys akharey hacoheyn v'ra'ah

לֹא־הָפַךְ הַנֶּגַע אֶת־עֵינוֹ

eyno et hanega' hafach lo

Once again as we pass through the sections of the *Torah* that deal with the issues of *tzara'at* - a skin affliction that our tradition teaches was *HaShem's* supernatural response to *lashon hara* - gossip, slander, speaking evil of someone - we find ourselves struggling to connect our modern world, when this phenomenon does not seem to be manifested, with the ancient texts. Much has been written - perhaps most famously by the Chofetz Chaim - about the evil of *lashon hara* and the need to avoid it and judge others favourably, but although Jewish writers speak eloquently about the damage that can be done by careless words, they have no certain remedy to offer for stopping the offence and repairing the damage. Certainly, taking time and trouble to develop better habits of speech, thinking carefully before opening one's mouth and developing rules for not making judgements of other peoples' words and actions will reduce the scale and spread of the problem and are - indeed - fully supported by the writers of the New Covenant Scriptures, but they are all external measures, addressing future infractions. What is needed is both a change of heart so that the thoughts and comments are never generated in the first place, rather than simply being suppressed and prevented from getting out, and a means of cleansing and forgiveness for past offences.

Our text provides a clue to the problem. The word הֻכַּבֵּס is an unusual verb form: a *hotpa'el* infinitive construct. The *hitpa'el* stem is used to indicate iterative or repeated action, something that is done again and again; the *hotpa'el* stem adds the passive quality, denoting repeated action being done to the subject. The root of the verb is כָּבַס, to wash, so that in this use, the word speaks of frequent and repeated washing. The person whose garment has been afflicted with *tzara'at* has washed it over and over again to remove the stain - as if it were persistent dirt or mould - but to no avail: the mark stubbornly remains fixed and unchanged.

We have a similar problem with sin, "because the Lord has a case against His people, even with Israel He will dispute" (Micah 6:2, NASB). And if Israel, how much more the nations of the world. How are we to get rid of the sin in our lives, to be able to be clean before God? God Himself wants to resolve the problem since He knows full well that we cannot do this ourselves; no matter how we try to remedy our behaviour, to remove the stain, it will not wash out. "'Come now, and let us reason together,' says the Lord, 'though your sins are as scarlet, they will be white as snow; though they are red like crimson, they will be like wool'" (Isaiah 1:18, NASB). How can God say this when He knows that no amount of talking on our part will bring this about? Because He has already provided the solution in Messiah Yeshua. We know that "it is the blood that makes atonement" (Vayikra 17:11, CJB) and "without the shedding of blood there is no forgiveness of sins" (Hebrews 9:22, CJB), so "the blood of His Son Yeshua purifies us from all sin" (1 John 1:7, CJB). So much so that the Scriptures tell us of a question and answer in John's apocalyptic vision: "'These people dressed in white robes - who are they?' ... 'These are the people who have come out of the great tribulation. They have washed their robes and made them white with the blood of the Lamb. That is why they are before God's throne'" (Revelation 7:13-15, CJB).

Towards the end of His ministry Yeshua told a parable about a wedding feast in order to describe the Kingdom of Heaven. After the original guests refused to come to the feast and the king's servants had filled the wedding hall with guests from the highways and byways, the king came to see that all was ready. "Now when the king came in to look at the guests, he saw there a man who wasn't dressed for a wedding; so he asked him, 'Friend, how did you get in here without wedding clothes?' The man was speechless. Then the king said to the servants, 'Bind him hand and foot and throw him outside in the dark!' In that place people will wail and grind their teeth, for many are invited but few are chosen" (Matthew 22:11-14, CJB). It is essential that we not only hear God's call and invitation to come into His kingdom but that we wear the clothes of the kingdom - robes washed in the blood of the Lamb!

Further Study: Zechariah 3:3-5; Revelation 22:14

Application: Are you wearing the right clothes for life in the kingdom of God? It is not enough to simply go along, join in the activities and talk the talk. As the priest inspected those with *tzara'at* to see if the blemish had gone, so the King inspects us to see if we are wearing the garments He has provided: the robes of righteousness, and they only come from knowing Yeshua and accepting His free gift of salvation.

מְצֹרָה ב׳

Metzorah - One with tzara'at - 2

(In an ordinary year this could read as Tazria/Metzorah 4)

Vayikra / Leviticus 14:13 - 20

Vayikra/Leviticus 14:13 He shall slaughter the lamb in the place that he will slaughter the sin-offering

וְשָׁחַט אֶת־הַכֶּבֶשׂ בִּמְקוֹם אֲשֶׁר יִשְׁחַט

yish'khat   asher   bim'kom   hakeves   et   v'shakhat

אֶת־הַחַטָּאת

ha'khatat   et

Having brought the lamb into the courtyard as a guilt offering (v. 12), the *cohen* is now to slaughter the lamb at the place where the sin offering is normally slaughtered. Rashi tells us that this is at the side of the altar, on the north, and then goes on to ask why the *Torah* had to say this in any case. In *parasha* Tzav (Vayikra 7:2) the *Torah* clearly states that the general rule is that the guilt offerings are slaughtered in the same place as the burnt offerings, which in turn is to be on the north side of the altar (Vayikra 1:11), so since the *Torah* doesn't waste words, Rashi's question seems appropriate. The answer seems to be that this offering is unique because the offerer and the offering have been 'placed' before *HaShem* at the entrance to the Tent of Meeting (14:11) - on the east - perhaps suggesting that the offering should be slaughtered there; this is why the *Torah* states that the slaughtering is to be done as usual where the other guilt offerings are slaughtered.

Such precision and attention to detail, particularly with regard to the Temple and its ritual is consistent throughout Scripture; perhaps no more strikingly than in the instructions and measurements for the 'new' Temple shown to the prophet Ezekiel. After being told to pay particular attention to all the details, Ezekiel's first observation is that the 'man' showing him the vision had "a measuring rod of six cubits, each of which was a cubit and a handbreadth" (Ezekiel 40:5, NASB). Every cubit measures not the usual eighteen inches, but is an extra three inches long, to make twenty one rather than eighteen inches. Then all the rooms and the overall building sizes are detailed: "the guardroom was one rod long and one rod wide" (v. 7), "the side pillars sixty cubits high" (v. 14), "the width from the front of the lower gate to the front of the exterior of the inner court, a hundred cubits on the west and on the north" (v. 19, NASB). As we now know, such a temple is many times the size of Solomon's temple and still much larger than that of Herod. The exact measurements serve not only as the building/architectural frame, but also as a specific sign of design: this is not to be a haphazard collection of rooms built as they are needed, or slowly growing over time. God has a plan and it to be built that way from the start.

In Matthew's gospel, which is the most marked for this characteristic, we find time and again the phrase "this happened in order to fulfil what was written", "all the words that the prophet said" and so on. Matthew is emphasising that Messiah didn't happen by accident. Yeshua wasn't just a good man and good teacher whom God used because He was there at the time. Yeshua is "the lamb slain before the foundation of the world" (Revelation 13:8, KJV) and everything that happened was "in accordance with God's predetermined plan and foreknowledge" (Acts 2:23, CJB).

Further Study: Matthew 21:1-17; Amos 3:6-7

Application: Why not spend a little while reasoning just how many things that happened in the week before Passover and including Yeshua's death and resurrection were designed and described beforehand by God.

תַזְרִיַ/מְצֹרָה ו׳

*Tazriya/Metzorah - She will conceive/One
with tzara'at - 6*

(In a leap year this could be read as Metzorah 4)

Vayikra / Leviticus 14:33 - 15:15

Vayikra/Leviticus 14:35 And he shall announce to the priest, saying:
"Something like an affliction has appeared to me in the house."

וְהִגִּיד לַכֹּהֵן לֵאמֹר כְּנֶגַע נִרְאָה לִי בַּבָּיִת:

ba'bayit liy nir'ah k'neg'a leymor la'koheyn v'higiyd

The word כְּנֶגַע - like an affliction, 'something' implied - seems to be
an unusual choice. Why should the house-owner not bring a definitive report
to the *cohen* so that remedial work can begin at once? Rashi points out the
first answer: it is the *cohen's* appointed responsibility to pronounce the
verdicts of 'clean' or 'unclean' after inspecting the markings in the house.
The sages hypothesise (Torat Kohanim, Tazria 1:9) that even if the *cohen*
should himself be unable to make the determination and need to be advised
by a *Torah* scholar exactly how to read and interpret the physical signs, the
procedure is that the scholar recommends that the *cohen* should, in his
opinion, say "this is clean" or "this is unclean", but that the legal change of
purity status takes place only when the declaration leaves the *cohen's*
mouth. For the house-owner, however well educated or versed in the
regulations of *tzara'at*, to make a determination is usurping the *cohen's*
authority. As Rashi says, "even if he is a *Torah* scholar, who knows that it is
certainly an affliction, he should not render judgement with a definitive
statement by saying, 'An affliction has appeared to me'; rather, 'Something
like an affliction has appeared to me'."

Both Rashi and the Sforno look into the following verse to deduce a
second answer to our question. Rashi comments that the *Torah* has pity by
allowing removal of the contents before the judgement is announced, so that
food, clothing, utensils and other personal possessions may be removed
from the house before it is sealed and the whole - house and contents -

declared unclean. The Sforno adds, "and they shall empty the house before the *cohen* comes; but he shall not come before this is done. In the interim, there will be time for the owners to pray and repent." The rabbis saw *tzara'at* as a supernatural sign of God's punishment for certain types of non-obvious sin; by allowing a window of time between the *tzara'at* appearing and the official declaration of impurity followed by the weeks of waiting and the cost of rebuilding and decoration or even the whole house being destroyed, the rabbis sensed God's mercy at work to prompt the guilty party to repent and be forgiven before sentence was carried out.

The Ba'al HaTurim explains that a *masoretic* note, 'ב next to the phrase נִרְאָה לִי means that it appears twice in the Tanakh: here and in Jeremiah 31:2 מֵרָחוֹק יהוה נִרְאָה לִי -*Adonai* appeared to me from afar. Even though the latter is speaking of God foretelling a time of blessing when He would restore Israel: "I have loved you with an everlasting love; therefore I have drawn you with lovingkindness. Again I will rebuild you, and you shall be rebuilt, O virgin of Israel! Again you shall take up your tambourines and go forth to the dances of the merrymakers. Again you shall plant vineyards on the hills of Samaria ..." (Jeremiah 31:3-5), NASB), the Ba'al HaTurim's lesson is that God is warning the people in advance of what is going to happen so that they have time to prepare and be ready for what He is about to do.

Nechama Leibowitz shares a telling quote from Rabbi Eliyahu Mizrahi: "I have learned from my Masters that the wording is not associated with the definition of purity and impurity. Rather, it serves as a moral lesson, i.e., even in the event of certainty about an impurity, one should declare it as doubtful. Thus our Sages have stated 'Teach your tongue to say: I do not know' (*b.* Berakhot 4*a*)". Leibowitz then adds the pithy observation: "This is particularly relevant to the modern news media and their tendency to present doubtful information as an established fact." It is an almost universal human habit to repeat and, in the process often to embellish, stories and anecdotes that we hear. Peoples' lives and reputations can be ruined by gossip and rumours based either upon a single misunderstood or misquoted remark, or oftentimes nothing more than supposition or idle speculation; sometimes even deliberate fabrication. The rabbis likened gossip to murder or character assassination because it can kill a person's life and, often, the person themselves due to the stress and embarrassment caused. Believers should play no part in spreading or even receiving gossip, whether from a stranger or a friend. We should only repeat or report what is certain truth. As James wrote "And the tongue is a fire, the very world of iniquity; the tongue is set among our members as that which defiles the entire body, and sets on fire the course of our life, and is set on fire by hell" (James 3:6, NASB), he picks up the same theme as the ancient rabbis who decided that *tzara'at* was the way in which God publicised and punished gossipers and slanderers. Yeshua spoke the same words when He said, "But what comes out of your mouth is actually coming from your heart, and that is what makes a person unclean" (Matthew 15:18, CJB).

Although *tzara'at* is held by the rabbis only to operate when the people of Israel are living in the land of Israel and in a theocracy where the priests administer the *Torah*, God is still just as concerned that damage is done today between people by habits of gossip. Yeshua warns believers that, "Moreover, I tell you this: on the Day of Judgment people will have to give account for every careless word they have spoken; for by your own words you will be acquitted, and by your own words you will be condemned" (Matthew 12:36-37, CJB). Neither is the context in which we speak any protection, for He follows that up with the warning that "Accordingly, whatever you have said in the dark shall be heard in the light, and what you have whispered in the inner rooms shall be proclaimed upon the housetops" (Luke 12:3, NASB). In a verse that speaks both inwards and outwards, the Psalmist cries, "Deliver my soul, O Lord, from lying lips, from a deceitful tongue" (Psalm 120:2, NASB); he needs to preserved against the effects of other peoples' lies and deceit, but he also needs to be protected from developing those same habits himself and being destroyed from within!

Given such a certain warning and exhortation, how should we govern our actions and conduct? All of us at some time or another have been guilty of, at best, careless or thoughtless speech; at worse, many of us have taken pleasure in passing on unflattering comments, criticism or reports of someone's behaviour or mistakes, possibly even originating them. We justify this either on the grounds that it is in the public interest that as wide a circulation as possible of that person's faults is made so that other people are not deceived or taken in by them, or because we are allowing the person to suffer from their own actions or words - often a thinly disguised form of revenge or getting one's own back. In the latter case, God simply forbids revenge, as Rav Sha'ul writes: "Never take your own revenge, beloved, but leave room for the wrath of God, for it is written, 'Vengeance is Mine, I will repay,' says the Lord" (Romans 12:19, NASB); as to the former, Yeshua said, "Woe to the world because of its stumbling blocks! For it is inevitable that stumbling blocks come; but woe to that man through whom the stumbling block comes!" (Matthew 18:7, NASB). Even passing on an opinion or unauthorised but true facts about people in prayer requests or prayer chains constitutes gossip. Once we become aware of our actions, we should make restitution where possible by apologising to the person concerned and repenting before God at the first opportunity.

Further Study: Psalm 34:5; 2 Peter 3:14

Application: Have you been caught out with this one? It is so easy that the enemy often uses it to trip us up and spoil our relationships with other people and with God. Think back and you'll most likely find at least one incident that you need to cover. Why not make a start right now and ask the Holy Spirit to give you a nudge before you open your mouth next time you're tempted?

מְצֹרָה 'ה

Metzorah - One with tzara'at - 5

(In an ordinary year this could be read as Tazria/Metzorah 6)

Vayikra / Leviticus 14:54 - 15:15

Vayikra/Leviticus 14:54 This is the law for all tzara'at and afflictions involving hair loss

זֹאת הַתּוֹרָה לְכָל־נֶגַע הַצָּרַעַת וְלַנָּתֶק:
v'lanatek hatzara'at nega l'chol ha'torah zot

    Coming at the end of a significant block of regulations (all of chapters 13 and 14) concerned with the various manifestations of *tzara'at* in people, buildings and clothing, and before moving on to the next topic, the four verses starting with this text form a summary of the preceding material. Levine comments that while the formulaic זֹאת הַתּוֹרָה - this is the law - "often serves to introduce a manual of practice, as in verse 2, here it serves as a concluding statement." Earlier in the chapter, the phrase introduces a sequence of ritual for a particular situation, the sanctification ritual; at this point it marks the end of the conversation on this topic block and is followed by the names only of all the conditions previously discussed.

    Hirsch, who translates וְלַנָּתֶק as "and for alopecia", suggests that the first two elements in the list of conditions are the most extreme forms, positively and negatively respectively, that the class of affliction takes, thus bracketing the following verses. Rashi, passing over the individual conditions, picks upon the two significant events in the course of the affliction: "which day renders him pure and which day renders him impure." Before and after, the person is ritually clean; in between he is ritually unclean; but Rashi sees the most important parts as the transition from one state to another and the ritual that accompanies or accomplishes the change. Sforno adds that "he who comes to instruct regarding the afflictions must know how to differentiate between two kinds of affliction even though they are of one class, as it says, 'between affliction and affliction' (D'varim 17:8)", suggesting that the *cohen* who makes the decision must have considerable expertise and experience.

Sforno's comment, however, also points to a larger principle: "two kinds of affliction even though they are of one class". Our text explicitly says that "this is the law for all *tzara'at* and afflictions". Though there are different manifestations with their own particular distinguishing marks, seen in different places or materials, and with a range of intensities, they are nevertheless all one class of item: *tzara'at*. As one basic item, therefore, there is one law that prescribes how it is to be treated from a ritual point of view. Like the *tzara'at*, that law takes different forms - a blemish on someone's head is clearly treated in a very different way from mould forming in the walls of someone's house - but the principles of repeated examination, isolation and purification apply in all cases.

People, on the other hand, try hard to distinguish between different classes of sin; they will talk of telling "white lies" as if this somehow makes breaking one of the Ten Commandments acceptable (cf. Matthew 19:18). The Roman Catholic church teaches a difference between mortal sins - which lose one's place in heaven - and venal sins - which supposedly result only in varying times of punishment or purification in purgatory. As human beings, we try to excuse much of the sin in our lives, areas where we fall short of the conduct and behaviour that God expects of us, as being only trivial in nature and so not significant to God. We use phrases such as, "God will understand" or "I'm sure God will overlook this" in order to justify what we think are only minor infractions of God's standards. Some will even go as far as shrugging their shoulders and accepting sin as part of the human condition, saying that it doesn't matter because that is why Yeshua came: to pay the price for our sin; "we can't help it and He knew it, so He came to fix the problem for us."

Oddly, that isn't how the Scriptures see things. Rav Sha'ul writes: "Now the deeds of the flesh are evident, which are: immorality, impurity, sensuality, idolatry, sorcery, enmities, strife, jealousy, outbursts of anger, disputes, dissensions, factions, envying, drunkenness, carousing and things like that, of which I forewarn you just as I have forewarned you that those who practice such things shall not inherit the Kingdom of God" (Galatians 5:19-21, NASB). Sins of a wide range of natures, including some that most people would not even consider to be sin, are all grouped together as "deeds of the flesh" and Rav Sha'ul is explicit that those who do them will not inherit the Kingdom of God. He is just as definite in another list, where he talks about people rather than actions: "Do you not know that the unrighteous shall not inherit the Kingdom of God? Do not be deceived; neither fornicators, nor idolators, not adulterers, nor effeminate, nor homosexuals, nor thieves, nor the covetous, nor drunkards, nor revilers, nor swindlers, shall inherit the Kingdom of God" (1 Corinthians 6:9-10, NASB). It would seem that God has a very black and white view of sin - something either is sin or it is not sin - and that any sin knowingly tolerated or practised prevents us from being in proper relationship with Him.

How are we supposed to move forward from here? Rav Sha'ul again: "Wretched man that I am! Who will free me from the body of this death?" (Romans 7:24, NASB). Our salvation lies in exactly this property. Our text from the *Torah* says: "this is the law for all *tzara'at*" and sin works in exactly the same way: "the wages of sin is death, but the free gift of God is eternal life in Messiah Yeshua our Lord" (Romans 6:23, NASB). Sin is sin and results in death, regardless of what it is; freedom from sin is freedom from sin, regardless of what it is: "Behold the Lamb of God who takes away the sin of the world" (John 1:29, NASB). We confess our sin, make appropriate restitution or reconciliation with the other people concerned, receive God's forgiveness by faith in Yeshua and have moved from darkness to light, from death to life, for "There is therefore no condemnation for those who are in Messiah Yeshua" (Romans 8:1, NASB).

Further Study: John 5:28-29; 2 Corinthians 5:16-19

Application: Do you find yourself excusing actions and habits in your life that you know in your heart would not please God? Get a life! Recognise them for what they are - sin - then repent, confess them to God and ask Him to forgive you. Job done; receive His forgiveness in Yeshua and move on - you have a life to live for Him, without sin. Go to it!

תַזְרִיעַ/מְצֹרָה ז׳

Tazriya/Metzorah - She will conceive/One with tzara'at - 7

(In a leap year this could be read as Metzorah 6)

Vayikra / Leviticus 15:16 - 33

Vayikra/Leviticus 15:16 ... and he shall wash in water all his flesh and he will be impure until the evening.

וְרָחַץ בַּמַּיִם אֶת־כָּל־בְּשָׂרוֹ וְטָמֵא עַד־הָעָרֶב:

ha'arev ad v'tamey b'saro kol et bamayim v'rakhatz

Never being one to shrink from discussing human biological functions where necessary, the *Torah* is midway through a set of rules for people who have various types of bodily emissions. Ranging from open wounds or sores to a woman's monthly menstrual flow, most categories of natural or exceptional loss are covered during the discussion. This particular verse concerns a male who has a loss of semen; Baruch Levine points out that this particular rule is amplified in Moshe's recapitulation of the *Torah* on the plains of Moab: "If anyone among you has been rendered unclean by a nocturnal emission, he must leave the camp, and he must not reenter the camp. Toward evening he shall bathe in water, and at sundown he may reenter the camp" (D'varim 23:11-12, JPS), but that in the same way as natural sexual intercourse (Vayikra 15:18), this regulation does not require a sacrifice: just washing and waiting until evening is enough to restore purity. Ibn Ezra stresses that the loss should be involuntary; deliberate loss - as, for example, by Onan, the son of Judah, who did not want to father a son in his brother's name (B'resheet 38:8-10) - is a specific offense.

Ibn Ezra goes on to clarify that "the reference to 'all his flesh' clearly indicates that it means his whole body." He is supported by Chizkuni, who says that he must wash in "enough water to contain his whole body, that is a quantity of water one cubit by one cubit by three cubits" - three cubic cubits! Rabbi Hirsch adds, "every tiny part of the body must come into direct contact with the water, no extraneous matter may be present on the body". Rabbinic practice is that when immersing in the *mikvah* a person should be completely naked. Gersonides makes the telling comment that, "All portions of the person's body must be immersed simultaneously; it is impossible to become partially clean. If any part of his body is unclean, he is completely unclean". The Psalmist, using the words that are echoed each year in the Passover Hagaddah, adds the thought: "Who may ascend into the hill of the Lord? And who may stand in His holy place? He who has clean hands and a pure heart" (Psalm 24:3-4, NASB). It is not enough to be clean on either the inside or the outside, both must be clean in order to enter God's presence.

Focusing on one particular Passover *Seder* - the last one that Yeshua celebrated with His disciples, we find the following narrative: "So He rose from the table, removed His outer garments and wrapped a towel around His waist. Then He poured some water into a basin and began to wash the feet of the talmidim and wipe them off with the towel wrapped around Him" (John 13:4-5, CJB). It was customary in those days for a servant to wash the feet of those who had arrived at someone's house, to remove the dust, sand and grit from travelling. The *seder* itself includes hand-washing so, since only Yeshua and the disciples were present, Yeshua Himself took the part of the servant and washed the disciples' feet. Simon Peter protests and, in spite of Yeshua's attempt to calm him down, bursts out: "You will never wash my feet!" (v. 8, CJB). He is concerned with the propriety of having Yeshua wash his feet; so much so that he nearly misses the real point of what is going on. Yeshua has to remind him, "If I don't wash you, you have no share with Me" (still v. 8). We who have the benefit of knowing Rav Sha'ul's priority for being "in Christ" might wonder why it was taking Peter so long to catch on, but suddenly he says, "Lord, not only my feet, but my hands and head too!" (v. 9, CJB) - if that's what's at stake, then he's all in. He must be all clean, not just his feet. Yeshua points out that, "A man who has had a bath doesn't need to wash, except his feet - his body is already clean" (v. 10, CJB). The disciples are already clean because they have been with Yeshua, they have believed in Him and He has cleansed them. Their lives over the last three years have been total immersion in ministry with Yeshua and learning from Him.

When becoming a believer, many people compartmentalise their lives. They do church with one part of their lives and they go to work or play sport with other parts of their lives, maintaining separate personalities and sets of behaviour and standards in each compartment. Sometimes this is unintentional - they don't even realise that they are doing it - and at other times, it is a deliberate mechanism to prevent changes or influence in one area of their lives affecting other areas. Some compartmentalisers think that everyone lives like that - they only see other believers in church space, so have no way of knowing that anyone else lives in a different way all the rest of the time. This is rather like washing just one sleeve of a shirt, or only one leg of a pair of trousers; it is clean, but the rest of the garment continues to be as dirty as it was before.

In order to be fully a believer in Yeshua, to experience His forgiveness for our sins, the power and freedom of the *Ruach* dwelling inside us and a certainty of resurrection with Yeshua, we have to be totally committed to Him. A body cannot be resurrected with just one arm, the opposite leg and a couple of ears - it is all or nothing. We must bring all of our lives to Yeshua and allow Him to be our Lord in everything that we are and everything that we do. We cannot hold things back, fearing that if we let Him touch this or that part of our lives then He may make changes that we don't want or wouldn't like. If He is not the Lord of all of our lives, then He cannot be our Saviour either. "Any city or house divided against itself shall not stand" (Matthew 12:25, NASB)!

Of course this is usually a process; at the moment of first faith, we may give over all that we can think of at the time. Then, as time goes by, we realise that we also need to invite Yeshua to take control of our emotions, our finances, our relationships, our jobs, our families; in fact, not to put too fine a point on it, He needs to be in charge of everything. This may take a while, as things come to light and He asks us to let go of more and more, but the process is critical. If we hold back and refuse to release something into His control then it becomes locked and our progress in getting to know Him and becoming like Him comes grinding to a halt; we give the enemy a foothold in our lives. We must be sure that we are true and full followers of Messiah Yeshua so that we know where we stand. He said, "He who is not with Me is against Me; and he who does not gather with Me scatters" (Matthew 12:30, NASB).

Further Study: Psalm 51:1-4; 1 Corinthians 6:11; Ephesians 5:25-27

Application: Today would be a good time to conduct a spiritual inventory and check for signs of compartmentalisation - are you holding on to an area of your life that you won't let Yeshua have? If so, then you need to start negotiations for hand-over and become united under His headship - a true citizen of the kingdom.

אַחֲרֵי מוֹת/קְדֹשִׁים

Acharei Mot/K'doshim - After the death/Holy Ones

Vayikra / Leviticus 16:1 - 20:27

- in leap years, the two *parashiyot* are read separately; in regular years, they are read together -

רִאשׁוֹן	Aliyah One	Vayikra/Leviticus 16:1 - 24
שְׁלִישִׁי	Aliyah Three	Vayikra/Leviticus 17:8 - 18:21
רְבִיעִי	Aliyah Four	Vayikra/Leviticus 18:22 - 19:14
שִׁשִּׁי	Aliyah Six	Vayikra/Leviticus 19:33 - 20:7
שְׁבִיעִי	Aliyah Seven	Vayikra/Leviticus 20:8 - 27

אַחֲרֵי מוֹת - Vayikra/Leviticus 16:1 - 18:30

שֵׁנִי	Aliyah Two	Vayikra/Leviticus 16:18 - 24
חֲמִשִׁי	Aliyah Five	Vayikra/Leviticus 17:8 - 18:5

קְדֹשִׁים - Vayikra/Leviticus 19:1 - 20:27

שֵׁנִי	Aliyah Two	Vayikra/Leviticus 19:15 - 22
חֲמִשִׁי	Aliyah Five	Vayikra/Leviticus 20:1 - 7

אַחֲרֵי מוֹת/קְדֹשִׁים א'

Acharei Mot/K'doshim - After the death/Holy Ones - 1

(In a leap year this could be read as Acharei Mot 1)

Vayikra / Leviticus 16:1 - 24

Vayikra/Leviticus 16:1 Adonai spoke to Moshe after the death of the two sons of Aharon

וַיְדַבֵּר יהוה אֶל־מֹשֶׁה אַחֲרֵי מוֹת שְׁנֵי

sh'ney mot akharey Moshe el Adonai vay'dabeyr

בְּנֵי אַהֲרֹן

Aharon b'ney

Many of the commentators draw attention to this verse because it appears to omit what the Lord said. The usual formulation is: "And the Lord spoke to Moshe to say, '...'"; this verse starts the formula but the next verse (v. 2) starts again with: "And the Lord said to Moshe ...". Rashi goes as far as to ask, "Why does the *Torah* say this?" Perhaps it can be explained by seeing the context in which this took place: Aharon's two sons, Nadab and Abihu, have been consumed by fire proceeding from the Lord after offering incense in a way or at a time that He had not commanded. At the same time Aharon is told not to mourn for his two sons, a fairly difficult task at a human level. The Lord wants to keep the channels of communication open with both Aharon and Moshe, so at this delicate moment He speaks to Moshe lest Aharon should feel that this is all too much.

The level of human resilience in the face of tragedy is truly remarkable - reflecting, perhaps, our origin created in the image of God (B'resheet 1:27). Job retained enough faith, control and composure when he heard that all his sons and daughters had been killed to say, "Naked I came from my mother's womb, naked I will return there. Adonai gave; Adonai took; blessed by the name of Adonai" (Job 1:21, CJB). When the Lord took the wife of the prophet Ezekiel, he obediently carried out God's instructions: "I spoke to the people in the morning, and that evening my wife died. So I did the following morning as I had been ordered" (Ezekiel 24:18, CJB).

God tests and refines us throughout our walk with Him as believers, even as He tested *Avraham Avinu* (B'resheet 22:1ff). "'Therefore', says Adonai-Tzva'ot, 'I will refine them and test them ...'" (Jeremiah 9:6, CJB); "I will refine them as silver is refined, I will test them as gold is tested. They will call on My name and I will answer them. I will say 'This is My people' and they will say 'Adonai is my God'" (Zechariah 13:9, CJB), God not only knows our strengths and weaknesses, but what He is working to accomplish in us so that, "No temptation has seized you beyond what people normally experience, and God can be trusted not to allow you to be tempted beyond what you can bear" (1 Cor 10:13, CJB), and "Beloved, do not be surprised at the fiery ordeal among you, which comes upon you for your testing, as though some strange thing were happening to you" (1 Peter 4:12, NASB).

On the contrary, we have to stay in touch with God throughout the process, drawing our strength and endurance from Him, as it says, "Cast your cares upon Him, for He cares for you" (1 Peter 5:7, NIV).

Further Study: Hebrews 12:7-13; D'varim 8:1-6

Application: Have you been through a testing time lately and perhaps lost sight of God in the process? Or do you perhaps feel a grudge towards Him that this is happening to you? Take comfort that it is all for our good as He grows the character of Messiah Yeshua in us. Why not talk to Him about it today.

אַחֲרֵי מוֹת ב׳

Acharei Mot - After the death - 2

(In an ordinary year this could be read as Acharei Mot/Kedoshim 1)

Vayikra / Leviticus 16:18 - 24

Vayikra/Leviticus 16:18 And he shall go out to the altar that is before the Lord

וְיָצָא אֶל־הַמִּזְבֵּחַ אֲשֶׁר לִפְנֵי־יהוה

Adonai lif'ney asher miz'beyakh el v'yatza

This instruction appears in the middle of the sequence of commands describing the ritual to be carried out on *Yom HaKippurim*, the Day of Atonements. The verb וְיָצָא, "he shall go out" attracts the attention of the commentators because Aharon is already in the Holy Place, and the "altar before the Lord" is the gold altar that is in the Holy Place. Has Aharon left the sanctuary and returned, or where was he that he "went out" to the gold altar? The overall flow of the text in the surrounding verses suggests that Aharon's preceeding action was inside the *parochet*, curtain, and that he is working his way out from the Most Holy Place, to the altar in the courtyard.

Rashi suggests that he is moving around inside the sanctuary, but moving out of the direct line between the gold altar and the curtain. Mizrachi and Sifsei Chachamim suggest that this is speaking of the circular movement that Aharon must make in order to put blood on the four horns of the altar.

Singer and song-writer Stephen Curtis Chapman has a song which speaks of going out, called 'Treasure Island'. Some of the words say: "And I'll go sailing out to Treasure Island / The Treasure Island that God's word can be / I raise the sail as I kneel to pray / Guided by the Spirit's gentle wind / I'll pray and make my way to Treasure Island"[6]. Talking about having a quiet time each morning, he is speaking of the need to withdraw from the normal day-to-day activities of life and spend time alone with God and His word. We find Yeshua doing the same thing: "After He had sent the crowds

---

6. CD: 'More to this Life' - Words and music by Stephen Curtis Chapman, © 1989 Sparrow Song / New Wings Music / Greg Nelson Music

away, He went up into the hills by Himself to pray" (Matthew 14:23, CJB). If Yeshua needed times apart in order to pray and connect with Father God, then surely we do too!

But there is actually more to it than simply time alone with God, as the words of the *Torah* hint. Aharon had to 'go out' in order to perform some of his service in the Tent of Meeting. Almost, he had to step outside himself and even the role was was playing - not just a man, but the anointed High Priest - he had to go out from normality in order to touch God. In some books, God is described as being 'entirely other'; strange words that don't make grammatical sense, but point to the fact that God isn't 'in' this world in the way that we are. He exists in the spiritual world that nevertheless touches and intersects with our physical world in many ways and places. What both Aharon the *Cohen Gadol* and Stephen Curtis Chapman found is that sometimes in order to experience God's presence, to draw near to the altar, to function before Him, one has to 'go out', step into the 'spititual' and simply follow God by faith and obey Him 'because'. When we do that, we find Yeshua, the Great High Priest, who has already charted our course, guiding our feet and leading us on in the Kingdom of God.

Further Study: Luke 6:12-13

Application: If you are comfortable and routine in your relationship with God, why not try stepping out and finding Him outside your normal experience. Look around you and see Him afresh in other people, times and places.

אַחֲרֵי מוֹת/קְדֹשִׁים ג'

Acharei Mot/K'doshim - After the death/Holy Ones - 3

(In a leap year this could be read as Acharei Mot 5)

Vayikra / Leviticus 17:8 - 18:21

Vayikra/Leviticus 17:8 Any man from the house of Israel or from the sojourner who will sojourn in their midst

אִישׁ אִישׁ מִבֵּית יִשְׂרָאֵל וּמִן־הַגֵּר אֲשֶׁר־יָגוּר

yagur asher ha'geyr oomin Yisrael mibeyt iysh iysh

בְּתוֹכָם

b'tocham

This phrase starts one of a series of prohibitions that apply equally to the Israelites and to the sojourners - aliens, strangers - that are dwelling in their midst. The phrase repeats several times in the rest of the chapter and makes a number of interesting points.

The first thing to note is the status of the sojourner. The noun גֵּר, from the root verb גוּר is not used for someone who is simply passing through, of strictly short-term or temporary residence. Israel today has many foreign workers, but most are only there for a season; they have a temporary visa for a few months or years and then they return home to their country of origin; they are not גֵּרִים, sojourners. The גֵּר is one who has settled in the Land - more properly, among the people of Israel - on at least a semi-permanent basis; he has cast his lot in with the community of Israel, to live and work with them. Many of the Jewish translations of the *Tanach* - the Artscroll edition, for example - use the word 'convert' or 'proselyte' in this text, perhaps because they are uncomfortable with the idea of Gentiles participating in sacrifice and worship of the God of Israel as Gentiles, or perhaps because they see the commitment to reside long-term in Israel as being something that only a convert would do.

That leads to the second point: the sense of the verb used. יָגוּר is in prefix form denoting incomplete action, often translated in the future tense in English. Even though God is here giving instructions to Moshe for Aharon and the priests to do and to teach the Israelites, He is including sojourners in the target audience. From God's perspective, it is already a certainty that those from the nations will join themselves to Israel and seek to worship Him; when Isaiah spoke of this (cf. Isaiah 56:3-8), he was simply repeating what God had already outlined in the *Torah*. The participation of Gentiles in worshiping the One True God - from choice, and not from any obligation - was not an afterthought, it was both expected and anticipated.

The third point is that the first regulation in the set, starting at verse 3, does not include the sojourners, thus making an important distinction: although the sojourners were subject to many of the rules and regulations that governed the community that they had joined, they were not universally obligated - the distinction between Jew and Gentile was maintained in spite of their close proximity. There was not one law universally applied in all matters to Israelite and sojourner alike. This is brought out by Rav Sha'ul: "For there is neither Jew not Gentile, neither male nor female, neither slave nor free, for you are all one in Messiah Yeshua" (Galatians 3:28). By deliberately choosing categories in which it was impossible to blur functional roles (for example, by men having babies), Rav Sha'ul emphasises our unity in Messiah, but our differences in calling and function within the body.

Further Study: Ephesians 4:11-16; John 3:16

Application: Are you unhappy with your position or status as a believer? Are you a Jew who wants to be a Gentile, or Gentile who longs to be Jewish? Relax and know that you are equally loved and wanted by God, a God who has deliberately made us different to worship and serve Him in variety and diversity, rather than bland homogeneity.

אַחֲרֵי מוֹת 'ה

Acharei Mot - After the death - 5

(In an ordinary year this could be read as Acharei Mot/Kedoshim 3)

Vayikra / Leviticus 17:8 - 18:5

Vayikra/Leviticus 17:9 And he does not bring it to the entrance of the Tent of Meeting to offer it to Adonai

וְאֶל־פֶּתַח אֹהֶל מוֹעֵד לֹא יְבִיאֶנּוּ לַעֲשׂוֹת אֹתוֹ

oto   la'asot   y'viyenu   lo   mo'eyd   ohel   petakh   v'el

לַיהוה

l'Adonai

Chapters 17-26 of Vayikra are known as the Holiness Code, a sub-section of the book that has a distinctive feel to it, but - according to Professor Richard Elliott Friedman - there is considerable disagreement as to exactly what the distinctiveness is, what it means, or how the text is to be distinguished from that which surrounds it. Thought by those who support the Documentary Hypothesis to be part of the source 'P', composed by priestly writers to preserve and describe the functioning of the cult at a central location, our verse is part of a doublet that states that anyone who offers burnt offerings or sacrifice to *HaShem* away from the Tent of Meeting will be cut off from the people. A more traditional reading of biblical history suggests that once the Tabernacle was built and erected, it became the central point of worship and sacrifice for all the people, first in the desert and then - once Israel has entered the Land - at Shilo. It was eventually succeeded by the Temple in Jerusalem, so that there was one static place in the country that served as a centre or focus for sacrifice, pilgrimage and ritual. Between the time of the Tabernacle at Shilo and the building of the Temple, however, the Rabbis interpret the texts to say that sacrifice to *HaShem* at בָּמוֹת, "high places", was allowed, while there was no one central place. See, for example, 1 Samuel 9:12.

It is certain that this text is more specific about sacrifice than texts earlier in the *Torah*. *HaShem* tells Moshe, "You shall make an altar of earth for Me, and you shall sacrifice on it your burnt offerings and your peace offerings, your sheep and your oxen; in every place where I cause My name to be remembered, I will come to you and bless you" (Shemot 20:24, NASB). Whilst this could be speaking of one central site for the people as they moved about through the desert on their journey to *Eretz Yisrael* - just as the patriarchs travelled throughout the Land, built altars and called upon the name of the Lord, so Israel's nomadic journeys would find the centre of their worship in the midst of the camp, wherever that might happen to be on any one day - it can also be read to imply that multiple sites of worship and sacrifice were envisioned. As the *Torah* proceeds, however, it becomes clear that only one site, one central location, is to be used: "Then it shall be, when you enter the Land ... that you shall take some of the first of the produce ... and go to the place where the Lord your God chooses to establish His name" (D'varim 26:1-2, NASB). Be it Shilo or the Temple, only one site is now in view.

Rabbi Samson Raphael Hirsch points out that the text is prohibiting sacrifice to God in any way that falls outside the scope of *Torah*. "Bringing an offering to God elsewhere than in the Sanctuary of the *Torah*, expresses the conviction that relation to God can be established, 'nearness' to God obtained, by other means than the *Torah*, without necessarily treading the path of God's Laws, that one can turn one's back on the *Torah* and still turn one's face to God." Or, in other words: someone who chooses to offer sacrifice somewhere else, is effectively saying to God, "I'll worship You how and where I please, regardless of what You have said, and You'll just have to put up with it and like it!" No wonder the *Torah* says that such a person is to be cut off, for as Hirsch continues, "thereby he has torn himself and his future out of Jewish ground as 'he shall be cut off from his people' actually declares to him and his descendants." If you reject God's word and commandments then you are rejecting Him, and rejecting Him means that you have no part in God's people, no relationship with Him - as Rav Sha'ul so poignantly described the Gentiles: "excluded from the commonwealth of Israel, and strangers to the covenants of promise, having no hope and without God in the world" (Ephesians 2:12, NASB).

It is in this context that we find Yeshua making what, in these days of tolerance and political correctness, is considered one of the more controversial - if not offensive - statements of our faith: "I AM the Way - and the Truth and the Life; no-one comes to the Father except through Me" (John 14:6, CJB). Whether for Jews or Gentiles, Yeshua is the way to approach God; He is the One who takes our prayers and service into the heavenly Tabernacle and presents them to God. As Israel's High Priest, even though the majority of our people still refuse to acknowledge Him as such, when Israel prays, they pray "in Him". The Gentiles, proclaiming Him as the Saviour of the World, draw near to God in Him and are grafted in to the olive tree, become children of Abraham by faith in Him. He is the Living

Torah, the way we come to God.

What should we say to people of other faiths or none? How should we respond to those who say that they have no need of church or religion, that they feel close to God in their gardens or on a mountain top? What reason can we offer to those who say they have already found peace with God through another of the world's religions? Simply this: "This Yeshua is the stone rejected by you builders which has become the corner stone. There is salvation in no-one else! For there is no other name under heaven given to mankind by whom we must be saved!" (Acts 4:11-12, CJB). It doesn't matter what others think, unless they come to God on His terms, according to this *Torah* - His Living *Torah* - then they are cut off; they have no relationship with Him. We tend to read that verse as saying that calling on Yeshua means that we must be saved - and that is true - but the converse is also true: there is no other name, no other creed, no other way that guarantees salvation than Yeshua. All those who build in other ways, on whatever foundation or with whatever materials, are effectively thumbing their noses at God and saying that they know best: God will just have to take what He can get. God's word declares that to be nothing but delusion!

Further Study: 1 Kings 8:27-30; John 20:30-31

Application: Are you trying to please God your way, by offering Him what you want or is convenient to you? Or are you seeking Him to find out what He wants from you so that you can please Him in obedience in Messiah Yeshua? Are you bringing your sacrifice to the Tent of Meeting, or still offering sacrifice upon your own high place?

אַחֲרֵי מוֹת/קְדֹשִׁים 'ד

Acharei Mot/K'doshim - After the death/Holy Ones - 4

(In a leap year this could be read as Acharei Mot 7)

Vayikra / Leviticus 18:22 - 19:14

Vayikra/Leviticus 18:22 You shall not lie with a male the lying down of a woman, it is an abomination.

וְאֶת־זָכָר לֹא תִשְׁכַּב מִשְׁכְּבֵי אִשָּׁה תּוֹעֵבָה

to'eyvah   isha   mish'k'vey   tishkav   lo   zachar   v'et

הִוא:

hiv

This week's text falls to one of the more controversial verses in the Scriptures, in both the Jewish and Christian worlds. Let us take a close look at the words and make sure that we know what it really says. According to Brown-Driver-Briggs, the word זָכָר can be used either as an adjective or as a noun; as an adjective, of humans only (cf. Jeremiah 20:15, B'Midbar 3:40,43), as a noun, of both animals and humans (cf. Shemot 13:12, Judges 21:12); in either case, it refers exclusively to those of the male gender. The verb תִשְׁכַּב comes from the root שָׁכַב, which has three principle meanings: to lie down to sleep, to lie down in death and to have sexual intercourse; teh subject matter of the chapter excludes the first, the second is clearly not in view and the third is the only possible reading in this context. מִשְׁכְּבֵי אִשָּׁה is a construct, the first word being the noun מִשְׁכָּב, which can mean either a sleeping place, such as a bed (1 Kings 1:47) or the act of lying with someone sexually; coupled with the second word - woman - the English rendering "the sexual lyings of a woman" seems clumsy but unambiguous. Finally, תּוֹעֵבָה, a noun which has the meaning of something abominable or detestable; Holladay gives as examples, D'varim 14:3: unclean animals as food, D'varim 32:16 and Isaiah 44:19: foreign gods, 1 Kings 14:24: detestable customs of foreign nations.

Coupled with the repetition, two chapters later in Vayikra 20:13, this text has traditionally been read as a prohibition of male homosexual activity and was joined by a rabbinic prohibition of female homosexual activity based on "Do not follow the ways of Egypt where you once lived, nor of Canaan, where I will be bringing you. Do not follow any of their customs" (Vayikra 18:3). A *midrash*, Sifra Aharei Mot 9:8, states that this refers to sexual customs, including same-gender marriages and is echoed in the Talmud (*b.* Yevamot 76*a*). Rav Sha'ul seems to speak clearly on the same issue: "in the same way, also the men abandoned the natural function of the woman and burned in their desire toward one another, men with men committing indecent acts and receiving in their own bodies the due penalty of their error"(Romans 1:27, NASB). He states that homosexuals would not even enter the Kingdom of God (1 Corinthians 6:9-10, 1 Timothy 1:9-10). The church has traditionally followed the synagogue in regarding both male and female homosexuality as being an abomination and a specific sin before God.

Richard Elliott Friedman suggests that תּוֹעֵבָה is a society-relative term and that the prohibition should therefore be conditioned upon the knowledge available to mankind and the degree of acceptance within society. He argues that since the current consensus of medical opinion is that homosexuality may be genetic and so not a matter of choice, it would be illogical of God to condemn people for an orientation that was not of their choice and beyond their control. Moreover, he posits that society no longer regards homosexuality as being an abomination, that its practice does not exclude a person from full participation in society and so concludes that while the original commandment may have been necessary or appropriate in a day when homosexuality was an abomination - as if to prevent fragmentation in society - it is no longer applicable in these days of greater tolerance. Needless to say, these views are not universally accepted and the debate in both faith communities will doubtless continue until Lord returns!

What is undeniable is that the gospel clearly prohibits discrimination, persecution or demonisation of homosexuals by heterosexuals or *vice-versa*. Much of the debate in recent years has been characterised by accusations of bigotry and hypocrisy, by name-calling and mud-slinging that is entirely inappropriate to those who claim to follow Messiah Yeshua. Arguments may and should be strongly held and passionately articulated, but only so far as we remember that we are all made in the image of God and are all accepted and loved in Messiah. "For we are not struggling against human beings" (Ephesians 6:12, CJB), "so it is with the fear of the Lord before us that we try to persuade people ... from now on, we do not look at anyone from a worldly viewpoint" (2 Corinthians 5:11,16, CJB). This is not to say that, depending on your point of view, the sin of homosexuality or the sins of intolerance and bigotry are acceptable before God - they are not; simply that while we are to hate the sin as God does, we are also to love the sinner.

Further Study: 1 Corinthians 13:1-7; Philippians 2:1-12

Application: However much we may disagree with other members of the Body of Messiah, we are called first of all to love one another as Messiah Yeshua loved us. Do you find this difficult in either this particular area or even some other matter? We should pray that the Lord will give us His love so that we may be able to overcome our differences and so be able to stand together on the common ground we have in Him.

קְדֹשִׁים ב׳

K'doshim - Holy ones - 2

(In an ordinary year this could be read as Acharei Mot/Kedoshim 5)

Vayikra / Leviticus 19:15 - 22

Vayikra/Leviticus 19:15 You shall not do wrong in judgement

לֹא־תַעֲשׂוּ עָוֶל בַּמִּשְׁפָּט

bamish'pat avel ta'asu lo

The noun עָוֶל, injustice or unrighteousness (the opposite of צְדָקָה, righteousness) is part of the family of words from the root verb עָוַל, to act wrongfully. Brown-Driver-Briggs suggests meanings that include violent acts of injustice and injustice of speech as well as injustice in general. Rashi applies the instructions to the legal context: "This teaches that a judge who perverts the judgement is called a wrong-doer, hateful and repulsive, banned and an abomination", while Hirsch applies it first to the community: not to misuse the position which the legislature and the judiciary give it over individuals; then to individual judges: demanding absolute equality of treatment of parties at law by the judge; and finally to every individual in their dealings and encounters with each other: to judge one's fellow favourably and to refrain from any form of gossip or slander.

Speaking of Messiah, Isaiah says: "He will not judge by what His eyes see or decide by what His ears hear, but He will judge the impoverished justly, He will decide fairly for the humble of the land" (Isaiah 11:3-4, CJB). The Branch, the Rod of Jesse, will be absolutely righteous in His judgement of rich and poor alike: no-one will be given places of honour or offered a seat while others are made to stand; no-one will be granted favour or given the benefit of the doubt because they can't afford a lawyer; no-one will be convicted or acquitted on the basis of a fine legal quibble. Those who are humble and poor - usually afflicted or oppressed by the strength or schemes of the wicked - will receive justice as ancient wrongs are reviewed and set right by the Judge who knows all things and all the thoughts of mens' hearts. It is partly to this that we allude when hearing of a death and we say the blessing *"dayan emet"*, the True Judge.

Zephaniah prophesied about God's people: "But I will leave among you a humble and lowly people, and they will take refuge in the name of the Lord. The remnant of Israel will do no wrong and tell no lies, nor will a deceitful tongue be found in the mouths" (Zephaniah 3:12-13, NASB). This is a high calling for us today - to walk out this vision - but since the prophet saw it, it must be achievable. It can be done! It is not only judges, leaders and others in positions of authority who are expected to do no wrong, but the whole people of God who are called to this high standard. Injustice in any of its forms: violence or oppression, speech or behaviour, discrimination or prejudice, is not to be found in those who are called by His name.

Further Study: Proverbs 10:23-25; Isaiah 53:7-9

Application: Since some level of preparation is usually required in order to avoid "spur of the moment" actions, which can sometimes turn out to be less righteous than we would otherwise want, now is a good time to plan how you can "do no wrong in judgement". Take the choice now, when you have the time to think about it, and your actions should then follow through.

אַחֲרֵי מוֹת/קְדֹשִׁים ו׳

Acharei Mot/K'doshim - After the death/Holy Ones - 6

(In a leap year this could be read as Kedoshim 4)

Vayikra / Leviticus 19:33 - 20:7

Vayikra/Leviticus 19:35 You shall not do iniquity in justice: in length, in weight or in volume.

לֹא־תַעֲשׂוּ עָוֶל בַּמִּשְׁפָּט בַּמִּדָּה בַּמִּשְׁקָל

bamishkal bamidah bamishpat avel ta'asu lo

וּבַמְּשׂוּרָה:

oovam'surah

Most of the Hebrew words in this verse need some explanation to allow us to see the scope of the command being given. The verb, תַעֲשׂוּ - a 2mp *Qal* prefix form from the root עָשָׂה - has two common meanings: to do or to make. Is iniquity something that we simply do, or is it manufactured or created by our actions? Put another way, is iniquity something that exists only temporarily while we are doing it, or do we make something that endures beyond the immediate time of our actions when we act in an incorrect way? The word עָוֶל, here translated iniquity, comes from a root עָוַל, meaning "to deal unrighteously, unjustly" in Hebrew; in Arabic it has the sense of turning aside or declining (Davidson). *Targum Onkelos* translates this using the adverb 'falsely': "Do not deal falsely in judgement". When iniquity is done, someone is denied justice and there is a turning away from righteousness. בַּמִּדָּה - in length - comes from the root מָדַד, to measure; a *masoretic* note ג׳ means that the word appears three times in the Hebrew Scriptures: here, Joshua 3:4 "a distance of two thousand cubits in measure" and 2 Chronicles 3:3 where the measurements for the length of the temple foundations are given. This, then, is a large scale land measurement. בַּמִּשְׁקָל - in weight - can also mean "in the act of weighing" and is derived from the verb שָׁקַל - to weigh, weigh out - which also produces שֶׁקֶל, the Israeli currency that was originally a weight of silver or other precious metal. Anything weighed in shekels therefore had to be of manageable size. Finally, וּבַמְּשׂוּרָה is a liquid measure of volume, roughly equivalent in modern-day terms to two or three teaspoonfuls, a small scale unit of measure. Obviously, this judgement applies to all categories of measurement, from the largest to the smallest and in all types of units.

Rashi points out that the first part of the verse, "You shall not do wrong in justice" is exactly the same wording as the admonition given to judges twenty verses earlier when they are told, "you shall not be partial to the poor nor defer to the great, but you are to judge your neighbour fairly" (v. 15, NASB). Why, Rashi wants to know, is the phrase repeated here and connected with units of measure, terms more associated with trade and the marketplace than with the legal profession? The conclusion he reaches is that *HaShem* regards the merchant and the judge in the same light because they are each performing judgement or arbitration in their different spheres. A businessman measuring cloth, weighing out spices or buying and selling parcels of land is no less required to be scrupulously honest and show no favour to man than a judge when hearing a case in court. Just as a judge who perverts justice is called a wrong-doer, hateful, repulsive, banned and an abomination so these terms should apply to a dishonest merchant. In the same way, Rashi observes, "he causes the five effects that are stated with regard to a judge: he contaminates the Land, and profanes the name of God; he causes God's presence to depart, and Israel to fall by the sword; he causes Israel to be exiled from their land (Vayikra 20:3, 26:30,33)". A corrupt judge and a dishonest business person are responsible for the same devastating destruction.

Rabbi Samson Raphael Hirsch sees the issue on an even wider, societal scale. "It is the justice of these things on whose correctness the honesty of human intercourse depends." Hirsch is concerned about the whole fabric of society, realising that theft and deceit among everyday commercial transactions are a reflection of the morality of everyday people and the expression of the values that society as a whole holds and enforces; it is a witness of who we are both as a people and as God's people. "This places the responsibility for and guard of, the honesty and legality of things in general in the conscience of every single person. Everyone is placed in charge of it, over it and any misuse of this power is just as great a wrong as a misuse of the legal power of a judge." It is not just that it is simple theft or robbery, which need not come at the end of a chapter concerned about holy living, but that the morality of having dishonest measures completely undermines the holiness of both the individuals and a whole society which tolerates such behaviour. A single act of dishonesty is easily dealt with; a society where dishonesty is endemic cannot be a witness to the holiness of God.

Peter, writing to the believers in the *Diaspora*, tells them, "As people who obey God, do not let yourselves be shaped by the evil desires you used to have when you were still ignorant. On the contrary, following the Holy One who called you, become holy yourselves in your entire way of life" (1 Peter 1:14-15, CJB). Our lives, as followers of Messiah Yeshua, are to be a living witness to God's character: honesty, integrity and holiness. Peter continues: "Keep your behaviour excellent among the Gentiles, so that in the thing in which they slander you as evildoers, they may on account of your good deeds, as they observe them, glorify God in the day of visitation" (1 Peter 2:12, NASB). If we behave in the same way as the people around us, allowing our morals and standards to be like theirs, then we too deserve the punishment that comes because of sin. Only when we are distinct in our behaviour, honest and upright in all our dealings, will the world notice that we are different. Even though they resent our behaviour, sensing that our honesty judges their dishonesty, yet they will have to acknowledge at the Judgement Day that we were a witness to them and give glory to God. Each of us, individually, wears the name of God on our sleeve and bears the reputation of the whole body of Messiah in our hands. We should live and act worthily of both.

Further Study: Amos 8:4-10; 1 John 3:1-3

Application: It is the little things that let most of us down; careless words or moments when we were not on guard. Why not ask God to help you with your "little things" today and keep you on your toes? When the small things are right, then you will have confidence to tackle the larger things.

קְדֹשִׁים ה'

K'doshim - Holy Ones - 5

(In an ordinary year this could be read as Acharei Mot/Kedoshim 6)

Vayikra / Leviticus 20:1 - 7

[This commentary does contain some material that a child might not understand or find comfortable. Parental guidance advised.]

Vayikra/Leviticus 20:3 For he has given from his seed to Molech in order to defile My sanctuary

כִּי מִזַּרְעוֹ נָתַן לַמֹּלֶךְ לְמַעַן טַמֵּא אֶת־מִקְדָּשִׁי

mikdashiy et tamey l'ma'an laMolech natan mizar'o kiy

The Hebrew text of this verse contains some interesting words. מִזַּרְעוֹ, here "from his seed", uses the noun זֶרַע from the root זָרַע. The root, similar to its cognate זָרָה, has the basic meaning of spreading or scattering, but usually has the more focussed meaning "to sow" or "to plant"; that gives the noun זֶרַע "seed" or in human terms, "issue, progeny" and another noun זְרוֹעַ as "arm", the limb that sows, or "strength, power", the force to sow. זֶרַע is used in a careful word-play in the story of the two older sons of Judah: "But Onan knew that the <u>seed</u> would not be his; so it was if he came to his [late] brother's wife, he would waste it on the ground lest he should give <u>children</u> to his brother" (B'resheet 38:9, emphasis added), to mean both semen, "human seed", and children or offspring. In this text, and confirmed by both tradition and archaeology, it is physical offspring - children - that are in view.

Levine points out that the verb נָתַן, normally translated 'give', "more precisely connotes devotion to a god" in this context. This a giving-over, a complete devoting of a person, animal or object to a god or for a religious purpose. This idea can be seen in B'Midbar 3:9 where Moshe is told to devote the Levites exclusively to Aharon and his sons the priests in the service of the Tabernacle, also in B'Midbar 8:16 where *HaShem* speaks of the Levites as devoted to Him in place of the first-born of the whole people of Israel. The word is also used in Micah - "shall I give my first-born" (Micah 6:7) - as one of the sacrifices that a man might consider (although forbidden and unwanted) offering to atone for his sin; like the ten thousand rivers of oil earlier in the verse, it is a rhetorical device to emphasise the futility of huge sacrifices compared to the simple obedience of walking humbly before God.

Lastly, מִקְדָּשִׁי, translated here as "My sanctuary" but also by others as "My holy things", comes from the root קָדֹשׁ, "to be holy or separate", which also also generates the adjective "holy" and the abstract noun "holiness". The prefix letter מ is used to denote a place or location in which the action of a verb takes place, so the noun - a place to be holy - takes the meaning of "sanctuary" or "holy place". This provides one of the ideas behind the concept of "claiming sanctuary" because many actions, such as taking revenge, were not considered "holy" so were not allowed within the defined area of holiness.

Rashi makes the connection to another text: "one who makes his son or daughter pass through the fire" (D'varim 18:10) and explains that "seed" or "offspring" in this verse not only covers immediate children but grand-children as well. He then borrows the phrase "when he gives his offspring to Molech" from the next verse (Vayikra 20:4) and broadens the prohibition to "unfit offspring". While no explanation of that term is explicitly given, two options are implied: either children of a forbidden union, such as between a *cohen* and a divorcee, or children born of incestuous or adulterous unions; or perhaps children born with a disability or handicap. In all cases, Rashi says, no child whatsoever is to be used in this way!

The Sforno, assuming that child sacrifice is so obviously forbidden that it does not need comment, turns the focus to the issue of defilement. Those who deliberately become טָמֵא or, worse still, bring defilement into the sanctuary of God are to be punished in the most severe way possible: they shall be put to death. This penalty serves three purposes: the offender himself is punished; the offender and his offence is excised from among the people; a deterrent is established to discourage others from the same offence. Any worship that is not of the One True God defiles both the name and the sanctuary of God, particular when performed by one who is supposed to be part of God's chosen people and called to be separate from the other nations, set apart for God alone.

Hirsch takes the debate to a moral plane that connects startlingly with modern medical ethics. "[Child sacrifice] subscribes to the idea which believes that the family, and especially the children, are under a power which reigns over their fate (טְמָא), a blind power which is inimical to the happiness of human well-being to which some of the children can be given over to save the rest of them." Although written in the 1860s and 1870s, it as if Hirsch can see medical science today preparing to allow genetic selection of embryos so as to permit parents to raise a child for the specific purposes of providing organs or other body-part donations for another older child. Apart from the devastating effect upon the donor child, who quickly realises that they have no value in themselves but only exist as a bank of spare parts for their sibling, this practice steps over two red-line boundaries. Firstly, it denies God's sovereignty in the area of life and death, usurping the right to create, shape and ultimately dispose of life in an arbitrary way without reference to the Creator Himself; secondly, it devalues the sanctity of life itself, rendering it as a simple commodity to be manipulated or controlled in a de-humanised way.

How do we draw the lines and boundaries in our lives to preserve and protect the holy: to be aware of the effect that our actions and attitudes have on those around us. If defiling or desecrating God's name resulted in someone being cut off from the community - Sforno suggests that since they have already been cut off from this world by their physical death, the penalty of being cut off by God must apply to the world to come - what does that say to us about the importance of not doing that today? While the big issues need us to give a clear moral lead and position, the smaller items of our every day speech and attitudes are just as important in portraying the character of God to our world.

Further Study: Jeremiah 32:26-35; 1 Corinthians 6:18-20

Application: Is it time to write some letters to your elected representatives in government to express your concern about the steady decline of medical ethics and the need to retake the high moral ground? Make sure that your own words and actions match that high moral position you are urging others to take so that you don't give your friends and family the wrong picture of God.

אַחֲרֵי מוֹת/קְדֹשִׁים ז׳

Acharei Mot/K'doshim - After the death/Holy Ones - 7

(In a leap year this could be read as Kedoshim 6)

Vayikra / Leviticus 20:8 - 27

Vayikra/Leviticus 20:8 And you shall observe My statutes and you shall do them; I am Adonai who is making you holy.

וּשְׁמַרְתֶּם אֶת־חֻקֹּתַי וַעֲשִׂיתֶם אֹתָם אֲנִי

aniy   otam   va'asitem   khukotay   et   ooshmartem

יהוה מְקַדִּשְׁכֶם:

m'kadishchem Adonai

    This verse stands at the head of a second, almost identical, set of rules about forbidden sexual relationships; the first being in chapter 18, verses 6-23. It is preceded by a section covering the abhorrent practice of child sacrifice that ends in one of the standard priestly authority formulas: "You shall consecrate yourselves therefore and be holy, for I am the Lord your God" (v. 7, NASB). Hirsch suggests that the כִּי - for, that, when, because - that starts the next verse introduces the list of commands that are being enjoined upon the Israelites; these are the statutes that are to be observed.

    The first verb, וּשְׁמַרְתֶּם - *Qal*, affix, 2mp, *vav*-reversive - is the most frequent way of issuing a command without using a direct imperative: "and you shall ...". The verb root is שָׁמַר, to guard, keep or observe - it speaks of taking care to keep and preserve as well as the practical observation. The second verb, וַעֲשִׂיתֶם - also *Qal*, affix, 2mp, *vav*-reversive - comes from the root עָשָׂה, most commonly to do or make, but sometimes - as here - with the sense of performing or carrying out. The third verb, מְקַדִּשְׁכֶם - *Pi'el*, participle, ms with a 2mp object pronoun suffix - describes *HaShem's* activities: He is the one who is making the people holy. The switch from the *Qal* to the *Pi'el* stem intensifies or strengthens the force of the action,

the meaning from "to be holy" to "to consecrate, to make holy, to
~~~s holy". Hirsch offers the translation, "leads you to holiness".

/badiah Sforno picks up a number of these threads when he
comme~nts in the first part of the verse, "In this manner, namely, that you
sanctify yourselves through separation from forbidden unions, you will
thereby keep and do them for future generations. But if you do not sanctify
yourselves, your descendants will doubtless also fail to be holy for they will
have been born in sin as the Psalmist says: 'Indeed I was born with iniquity;
with sin my mother conceived me' (Psalm 51:7, JPS)". One generation will
lead to another and the children of a forbidden relationship will already be in
sin before they start. The Sforno then balances that by commenting to the
second part as if *HaShem* were still speaking: "For in truth, I have
prohibited forbidden unions to sanctify you to My service." He seems to see
the two parts of the verse working together, but is he confused about who is
doing what and why?

Where, then, is the cause and effect in the text? Is this a human action
to separate ourselves from "sin" so that we become holy in order to serve
God? Has God provided the rules and the "obedience" mechanism for us to
demonstrate and practise our holiness as we try to become like Him? Or is it
that God is the one who declares or appoints people to be holy and that our
subsequent behaviour then flows from that state of holiness? We appear to
have two ways of reading the verse: either the actions create the holiness, or
the holiness generates the actions. Somewhat inconveniently for our minds,
because we like to resolve such apparent contradictions one way or the
other, rather than holding two seemingly opposite ideas in tension, the Bible
makes it plain that both are in fact true.

At a physical level, on the one hand, our set-apartness for God comes
directly from our disengagement from the ways of the world and our refusal
to participate in patterns of sin and destructive behaviour; our level of
holiness is in direct proportion to the level of separation that we manage to
achieve. It is God's laws that provide the standard that we need to keep and
that delineate the types of activity in which we may or may not participate.
Other people sense the different way in which God's people conduct
themselves, the way they speak, the love they show and so know that we
belong to God. Rav Sha'ul's letters contain two distinct but very similar lists
of behaviour and lifestyles that clearly demarcate those who are in the
Kingdom of God from those who are not (1 Corinthians 6:9-11, Galatians
5:19-24). A steady development of good habits and practices makes the
routine daily observance easier and our kingdom responses become
automatic as we grow more like Yeshua.

At a spiritual level, on the other hand, we know that simply keeping
rules from an external point of view leads to a lifeless and sterile existence
with no love or grace. Change needs to come from within as the holiness

that God has given us spreads from the inside out. God has certainly given us the rules that govern our behaviour, but these are meant to be seen as patterns and habits that those who are already part of the kingdom should naturally develop as they move in God's grace and get to know Him better. As our hearts become more attuned to His, as we learn to hear the *Ruach* speaking and nudging, then our outward behaviour will fall in step and the holiness that we already have will become apparent to others.

Theologians have two words that they use to name these processes: justification and sanctification. Justification is when we are declared "right" before God; this is seen as a single moment in time when we become part of the Kingdom of God, our past sins are forgiven in Messiah Yeshua and we are marked as righteous. Yeshua's words speak of this moment: "He who hears My word, and believes Him who sent Me, has eternal life, and does not come into judgment, but has passed out of death into life" (John 5:24, NASB); that passage from one legal state to another is the key concept. Rav Sha'ul says it again: "Therefore, there is no longer any condemnation awaiting those who are in union with the Messiah Yeshua" (Romans 8:1, CJB). On a judicial basis, the believer in Messiah has changed status from being a sinner, at odds with God and an object of His wrath, to being a child of God, a fellow-heir and citizen of the Kingdom of Heaven and - in Yeshua - beloved by God for His sake.

On the other hand, verses such as Yeshua's assurance to the scribe that "You are not far from the Kingdom of God" (Mark 12:34, CJB), and Rav Sha'ul's "work out your salvation with fear and trembling" (Philippians 2:12, NASB) speak of the process of sanctification: being conformed to the image of Yeshua, which is clearly a transformative process and takes time. Our lifestyles and habits do not change overnight and as we come to know Yeshua and His words better, so we come around into line and are "made" holy. During this process we will, of course, continue in some old habits that will eventually change but in the meantime cause us to sin; repentance and forgiveness are necessary to restore our relationship with God, but sins committed at this time do not alter our judicial status, provided always that they are dealt with.

Moshe, therefore, in our text above is speaking of both these things. Firstly, God had already justified the Israelites (by bringing them out of Egypt, through the Sea of Reeds and declaring them to be a holy nation and a kingdom of priests at Mt. Sinai), so they were now expected to live as members of His community, observing His standards for proper relationships and ways of conducting themselves - their status should lead to their actions. Secondly, however, God was still sanctifying them by urging them to observe the rules that He had provided; they needed to engage with those rules and live them out in community for the effect to be seen - their actions would lead to practical holiness.

As believers in Messiah, we are called to participate in those same processes today. God has declared "if anyone is in Christ, he is a new creation; the old has gone, the new has come!" (2 Corinthians 5:17, NIV), so we are called to live out that life of holiness by observing His commands such as "A new commandment I give to you, that you love one another, even as I have loved you, that you also love one another" (John 13:34, NASB) and "Be angry and do not sin; do not let the sun go down on your anger" (Ephesians 4:6, ESV); both intensely practical and examples of being a commanded people, subject to rules and obligations as a result of knowing God. At the same time, Yeshua says, "But the one who endures to the end, he shall be saved" (Matthew 24:13, NASB), showing that we are clearly in process and that our efforts are necessary to ensure arrival at the desired destination. In either case, Rav Sha'ul is clear that "I am sure of this, that He who began a good work in you will bring it to completion at the day of Jesus Christ" (Philippians 1:6, ESV).

Further Study: James 1:22-25; Hebrews 12:14

Application: Whether a new believer or a seasoned campaigner in the Kingdom of God, we all have work to do in reaching our goal and cooperating with God to make us into the image of His Son, Yeshua. If you have lost sight of that purpose, why not reconnect with God today and find out what is next on His "to-do" list in your life?

Emor - Say

Vayikra / Leviticus 21:1 - 24:23

רִאשׁוֹן	Aliyah One	Vayikra/Leviticus 21:1 - 15
שֵׁנִי	Aliyah Two	Vayikra/Leviticus 21:16 - 22:16
שְׁלִישִׁי	Aliyah Three	Vayikra/Leviticus 22:17 - 33
רְבִיעִי	Aliyah Four	Vayikra/Leviticus 23:1 - 22
חֲמִשִׁי	Aliyah Five	Vayikra/Leviticus 23:23 - 32
שִׁשִּׁי	Aliyah Six	Vayikra/Leviticus 23:33 - 44
שְׁבִיעִי	Aliyah Seven	Vayikra/Leviticus 24:1 - 23

Emor ~ Say ~ 1

Vayikra / Leviticus 21:1 - 15

Vayikra/Leviticus 21:1 "Say to the Kohanim, the sons of Aharon, and you shall say to them ..."

אֱמֹר אֶל־הַכֹּהֲנִים בְּנֵי אַהֲרֹן וְאָמַרְתָּ אֲלֵהֶם
aleyhem   v'amar'ta   Aharon   b'ney   ha'Kohanim   el   emor

The first thing we notice about this text is that the *Torah* appears to be redundant. Who, after all, are the priests if not the sons of Aharon? There are several ways of handling this; the first is to point out that just as with the phrase בְּנֵי יִשְׂרָאֵל, the sons or children of Israel, בְּנֵי אַהֲרֹן can be a collective plural for the children of Aharon, so that it is necessary to say "the priests" to mean only the male children, i.e. sons of Aharon. Another approach is to remember that when the tribe of Levi is numbered to count those eligible to serve in the Tent of Meeting (B'Midbar 4:1-3), only those between the ages of thirty and fifty actively serve; so our text may be emphasising that all the sons of Aharon are included, not just those currently serving as priests in the Tent of Meeting.

The second thing we notice is that instead of the usual combination of 'speak' and 'say', this text uses the verb אָמַר, say, twice. The Rabbis deduce from this that the second verb is to be included in what Moshe is to say to the sons of Aharon, thus instructing them to say it in turn to their sons. This reflects the familiar concept within Judaism of passing on the heritage in generations, from father to son, parents to children. As believers, we can see this not only in the sense of physical generations but also spiritual generations as we pass on the faith to those around us.

Rav Sha'ul wrote to Timothy, "And the things you heard from me, which were supported by many witnesses, these things commit to faithful people, such as will be competent to teach others also" (2 Timothy 2:2, CJB). See the number of generations at work here: Rav Sha'ul, Timothy, the faithful people and the others who would be taught. That's four spiritual generations. What Rav Sha'ul is really saying is that it isn't enough just to teach people information, you also have to impart to them the need to teach others; that teaching others is just as much a part of the package as the information itself. Our abilities as teachers can only be assessed when we see our pupils not only teaching their pupils but encouraging them in turn to teach the people they come into contact with.

Our text from the *parasha*, then, starts a chain of instruction from the priesthood - all those down through the generations who would serve as priests - concerning ritual purity and contact with corpses. This instruction was not only to be a way of life for the priests but was to be passed on from father to son, generation to generation, so that the whole priesthood would know how God expected them to behave in contact with death. How much more should we, as believers in Messiah Yeshua, set apart and holy for Him, model that faithful transmission of conduct and behaviour.

Further Study: Shemot 12:25-28; 1 Peter 3:15-16

Application: How good are you at communicating the important concepts of the faith to those around you and, in particular, your children? Could the process be improved by a course of study, spending more time with the Lord yourself, or simply speaking out when the opportunity arises?

אֱמֹר ב׳

Emor - Say - 2

Vayikra / Leviticus 21:16 - 22:16

Vayikra/Leviticus 21:17 A man from your descendants, to their generations, who has a blemish ...

אִישׁ מִזַּרְעֲךָ לְדֹרֹתָם אֲשֶׁר יִהְיֶה בוֹ מוּם
moom vo yih'yeh asher l'dorotam mizar'acha iysh

Here is an important admission from the *Torah*: priests can have blemishes! The next verses (vv. 18-21) state that a man who has a blemish may not draw near to serve in the *Mishkan*, and list some of the conditions that constitute a disqualifying blemish. Rashi connects this to Malachi 1:8 "Try offering [a sick] animal to your governor and see if he would be pleased with you" (CJB). The priesthood, although all of different sizes and shapes - as men are - had to be physically unblemished, like the sacrifices they offered, in order to be the reflection of God for the people. And yet here the *Torah* accepts that there will be children born to the descendants of Aharon who will have some physical defects from birth - that is, beyond their control. Even though Aharon and his sons were to be the "priests for ever" before the Lord, He was not going to protect them from the normal human conditions that affected all the other Israelites. *HaShem* wasn't creating a strain of super-humans who never caught a cold or suffered from illness or disease - the priests were to be just like everyone else.

In Second Temple times, there was a common belief that physical deformity or disablement was the result of sin, either on the part of the person themselves or their parents. This is why we find the disciples asking Yeshua, in the case of a man blind from birth, whether he or his parents had sinned. Yeshua's response shocked them: "His blindness is due neither to his sin nor to that of his parents; it happened so that God's power might be seen at work in him" (John 9:3, CJB). God never promised our people that we would always be healthy and live long, sickness-free lives. He certainly did say, "If you will give earnest heed to the voice of the Lord your God, and do what is right in His sight, and give ear to His commandments, and keep all His statutes, I will put none of the diseases on you which I have put on the Egyptians"

(Shemot 15:26, NASB), but that's not the same thing as "no sickness" which some people assume. Let's face the truth: bad things do happen to good people - so that God's power might be seen at work in them!

The writer to the Hebrew goes on to talk about Yeshua, "Therefore, since the children share a common physical nature as human beings, He became like them and shared that same nature" (Hebrews 2:14, CJB). Yeshua became like us "in every respect" (v. 17) so that He shared our human fabric and frailty; "in every respect He was tempted just as we are, the only difference being that He did not sin" (Hebrews 4:15, CJB). As both the priest who offered Himself as a sacrifice, and that perfect sacrifice for our sin, Yeshua had to be both physically and spiritually pure. Yeshua was absolutely *glatt kosher* in every respect. Not only did He bear our diseases (Isaiah 53:4) and the punishment for our sin (Isaiah 53:5) but He did so having resisted all temptation in His own life.

Further Study: Psalm 103:3-5; Matthew 8:16-17

Application: If you face challenges in your life, be they physical, mental or spiritual, know that Yeshua has been there before you and for you. As believers, we can and will have blemishes, but it is so that God's power might be seen in us and Yeshua makes us acceptable in God's sight as He is perfect in and for us.

אֱמֹר ג׳

Emor - Say - 3

Vayikra / Leviticus 22:17 - 33

Vayikra/Leviticus 22:20 Any that have a blemish you will not offer

כֹּל אֲשֶׁר־בּוֹ מוּם לֹא תַקְרִיבוּ

tak'riyvu lo moom bo asher kol

The Sforno is concerned that this and the preceding verse speak about animals for sacrifice that might have a blemish. He connects the need for the sacrifice to be perfect with God's own perfection: "The Rock! His work is perfect, for all His ways are just; a God of faithfulness and without injustice, righteous and upright is He" (D'varim 32:4, NASB). In particular, although all sacrifices are required to be without defect, the offerings of major holiness (e.g. for the burnt offering, the sin offering and so on) must be both male and without blemish, and the following verses list many defects that disqualify cattle and sheep from being suitable for sacrifice although (see v. 23) some animals with minor blemishes may be accepted for freewill offerings because they are not offered on the altar.

Sforno also makes the obvious connection to the opening of the book of Malachi: "when you present the blind for sacrifice, is it not evil? And when you present the lame and sick, is it not evil?" (Malachi 1:8, NASB). "'I am not pleased with you,' says the Lord of Hosts, 'nor will I accept an offering from your hand'" (v. 10, NASB); "'you bring what was taken by robbery, and what is lame and sick; so you bring the offering! Should I receive that from your hand?' says the Lord" (v. 13, NASB). Even a human governor would not accept defective animals at his table, so how much less will God accept defective sacrifices or offerings from us.

As the *Cohen Gadol*, Aharon had to offer a sacrifice for himself before he could offer one on behalf of the people; this is why *Yom Kippur* is really *Yom HaKippurim*, the Day of Atonements: first Aharon, then the altar and then the people. But that, as the writer to the Hebrews tells us, was only a temporary situation. The prophets tell us of God's search: "Run to and fro through the streets of Jerusalem, look and take note! Search her squares to see if you can find a man, one who does justice and seeks truth, that I may pardon her" (Jeremiah 5:1, ESV). "I sought for a man among them who should build up the wall and stand in the breach before Me for the land ... but I found none" (Ezekiel 22:30, ESV). What was God to do? How could He present an offering that would be acceptable? "He saw that there was no man, and wondered that there was no-one to intercede; then His own arm brought Him salvation and His righteousness upheld Him" (Isaiah 59:16, ESV).

To fulfill the *Torah*, God's own offering had to be perfect. John the Immerser said: "Behold, the Lamb of God that takes away the sin of the world" (John 1:29, ESV). God sent "His own Son in the likeness of sinful flesh" (Romans 8:3, ESV); "For our sake He made Him to be sin who knew no sin, so that in Him we might become the righteousness of God" (2 Corinthians 5:21, ESV).

Further Study: Hebrews 2:14-18; Galatians 3:13-14

Application: Do you look at yourself and think: I just have too many faults and blemishes - I can never please God? Then take heart - God has already done it for you; knowing us even better that we do ourselves, He Himself has rescued us and offered Himself - in Yeshua - as our sacrifice.

Emor - Say - 4

Vayikra / Leviticus 23:1 - 22

Vayikra/Leviticus 23:2 These are the appointed times of Adonai ... these are they: My appointed times.

מוֹעֲדֵי יהוה ... אֵלֶּה הֵם מוֹעֲדָי:
mo'aday heym eyleh ... Adonai mo'adey

This verse starts the chapter containing the full feast sequence for a whole year, bar the later additions of Purim and Hanukkah. They are known as הַמּוֹעֲדִים, the feasts or appointed times, twice here in this verse as "the feasts of the Lord" and "My feasts". Derived from the root יָעַד, which according to Davidson means "to appoint, as a place or time, to betroth", the festivals are more than a holiday but carry the sense of being a divine appointment where - by agreement - God and His people meet together, both to spend time in each other's company and also to conduct spiritual business: the offerings of worship and sacrifice. By the repetition of the word in this verse, the text emphasises both the purpose and the ownership of these times: God has appointed these times and they belong to Him; while the people will enjoy coming together and meeting their friends and relations, the main object is for the people of Israel - as a people - to meet with God and - as a people - to worship Him.

Sforno makes two points about this verse. First, he talks about what people will actually do on or during the day. Noting that some festivals require a complete abstention from all work, while others require only a cessation of servile work, he goes on to ask how the day is supposed to be spent. Perhaps with children in mind - for although adults may be able to concentrate for long periods of time, it is children who are likely to find a long serious day more of a struggle, if not a burden - he draws attention to a debate in the Talmud between Rav Eliezer and Rav Judah. Quoting from two verses: "on the seventh day there shall be a solemn assembly to the Lord your God" (D'varim 16:8, NASB) and "on the eighth day you shall have a solemn assembly" (B'Midbar 29:35, NASB) Rav Judah concludes that the days are to be divided: "devote half to God and half to you" (*b*. Pesachim

68b). This is taken to mean that although half the day should be spent in worship and study, half the day should also be spent on family relationships: visiting friends and family, playing with children, simply relaxing and having family time time together before the LORD in the time that He has set apart for us.

Sforno's second point concerns the difference between God's appointed times, which He desires, and "mundane gatherings devoted to the transitory pleasures of men." Whereas the former are to be proclaimed as holy convocations, days set apart by God and including time to be used for study and worship, Sforno quotes from the prophet Isaiah: "I hate your new moon festivals and your appointed feasts, they have become a burden to Me" (Isaiah 1:14, NASB, emphasis added). From this we learn two things - that the feasts of the LORD are of greater significance than those called by men, and that the time must be set apart or dedicated to God even if we use part of the time to relax and enjoy ourselves. Prayer meetings should be meetings where people pray, not just meet, gossip and schmooze; worship times should feature significant worship, not just tuning up, rehearsal and chit-chat between a few nice songs. Social activity is essential and God intends us to have plenty of it, but the focus is supposed to be on Him. He knows that when we worship, pray and study, putting Him first both in our individual lives and in our times together as His people, then the rest of our lives - together and individually - will be in the right proportion.

Rav Sha'ul wrote, "So don't let anyone pass judgement on you in connection with eating and drinking, or in regard to a Jewish festival or Rosh Chodesh or Shabbat" (Colossians 2:16, CJB). These things are all a question of calling and are not to be the subject of criticism between one believer and another. Jewish believers in Messiah are called to observe the Feasts of the Lord as part of our covenant responsibilities before God as a part of the Jewish people - God's chosen people - the remnant of faith within the Jewish community today. Gentiles, unless living within and part of a Jewish community, are not called to observe the Feasts of the Lord although they are welcome to participate by invitation; and by so doing, to give a powerful testimony of unity in the body of Messiah of Jews and Gentiles worshipping together. However the Feasts are kept, let them focus on God first and also allow time for celebration, rejoicing and play!

Further Study: Lamentations 1:4; Nahum 1:15; 1 Corinthians 10:31-33

Application: Are you consistent in setting time aside for the Lord? Do you allow for both study and worship time as well as relaxation and play time before Him? Do you make specific provision to include children and young adults in both worship and play on those days? Ask God to show you the balance He wants in your life and in your congregation.

Emor - Say - 5

Vayikra / Leviticus 23:23 - 32

Vayikra/Leviticus 23:24 It shall be for you a day of rest, a remembrance of the sound of a shofar

יִהְיֶה לָכֶם שַׁבָּתוֹן זִכְרוֹן תְּרוּעָה

t'ru'ah   zichron shabbaton lachem yih'yeh

Contrary to popular belief, the *Torah* does not explicitly command that the *shofar* should be blown on *Yom Teruah*, the day of blowing, more frequently known by our people as *Rosh HaShana*. The only specific *shofar* blowing that is commanded is two chapters later: "On the tenth day of the seventh month, on Yom Kippur, you are to sound a blast on the shofar; you are to sound the shofar all through your land; and you are to consecrate the fiftieth year, proclaiming freedom throughout the land to all its inhabitants" (Vayikra 25:9-10, CJB). Blowing the *shofar* is a requirement to announce the Jubilee Year. Comparing our verse with the parallel verse in B'Midbar - "In the seventh month, on the first day of the month ... it is a day of blowing for you" (B'Midbar 29:1) - the rabbis deduced that since this text speaks of remembering the sound in the same phrase as *shabbat*, whereas that text mentions blowing without referencing *shabbat*, the *shofar* was to be blown when *Rosh HaShana* fell on a weekday, but it was only to be remembered when it fell on a *shabbat*.

Rashi reminds us, "a remembrance of verses of remembrances and verses of *shofars*", that on *Rosh HaShana* we not only blow the *shofar*, but in the *Rosh HaShana* liturgy we recite verses that refer to *shofar* blowing and verses that speak of remembrance or remind God of His promises to us. "R' Abahu said: Why do we blow with a *shofar* of a ram? The Holy One, Blessed be He, said: 'Blow before Me using a *shofar* of a ram so that I will remember for your sake the binding of Yitz'chak the son of Avraham and I will consider it for you as if you had bound yourselves for Me'" (*b. Rosh HaShana* 16a).

The Ba'al HaTurim points to a *masoretic* note indicating that the word זִכְרוֹן is only used three times in the Hebrew Scriptures: here,

Ecclesiastes 1:11 and 2:16. He suggests that together these three refer to the three categories of people and judgements that are part of the traditional theme of the High Holy Days: the wise and the wicked being judged on *Yom Teruah* and written immediately into the Book of Life and the Book of Death respectively, being remembered and then dealt with by God; the third - and largest - group being held in remembrance until they are judged ten days later on *Yom Kippur*. Sforno, picking up another traditional *Rosh HaShana* theme, remembering that God is particularly thought of during the *Days of Awe* as sitting on the throne of justice (see *b. Rosh HaShana 8b*), uses the word תְּרוּעָה - from the root רוּע, to cry aloud, to sound the trumpet or alarm, to shout for joy (Davidson) - to link to "Sing for joy to God our strength; shout joyfully to the God of Jacob" (Psalm 81:2); on whichever day *Yom Teruah* should fall, we can always remember God's sovereignty and rejoice before Him that our days are in His hands, that He is a just and faithful God.

The Jewish people are noted for our ability to remember past events from our history: the destruction of the Second Temple; the crusades; the Expulsion from England (1290), Spain (1492) and many other countries; the pogroms and - in more recent times - family members who died in the Holocaust. We light *yarhzeit* candles on the anniversary of a close relative's death; we celebrate the feasts - at God's command - to remember creation (*Shabbat*), the Exodus from Egypt (*Pesach*), the giving of the *Torah* at Sinai (*Shavuot*) and God's provision for our people in the wilderness (*Sukkot*), each one on its own special day. Portions from the Scriptures are read every day in the synagogue services to remind us of the mighty acts that God wrought on our behalf: שִׁירַת הַיָּם - the Song at the Sea, who He is; the שְׁמַע - the LORD our God is One, and the commands He has given us: making *tzitzit* - tassels - on the corners of our garments. All sorts of practical things to say and do to remember important moments or words. This is the context that enables Rav Sha'ul, when giving instructions for the Lord's Supper to a Gentile church who were less familiar with the Jewish ways of doing and remembering, to say, "For as often as you eat this bread and drink the cup, you proclaim the death of the Lord, until He comes" (1 Corinthians 11:26, CJB).

How, then, should we observe the "day of blowing" and what should we remember? We should be sure to blow or hear being blown a *shofar*; we should remember that Yeshua Himself started His earthly ministry with the words, "Repent, for the Kingdom of Heaven is at hand" (Matthew 4:17) and we should repent not only for ourselves but as a part of the larger family of Israel - like Daniel (Daniel 9:3 ff.) and Nehemiah (Nehemiah 1:4 ff.); we should be remembering and anticipating Yeshua's return. Speaking of that time, Yeshua said, "[The Son of Man] will send out His angels with a great shofar blast and they will gather together His chosen people from the four winds, from one end of heaven to the other" (Matthew 24:31, CJB), which is probably a reference to the prophecy of Isaiah: "On that day a great shofar will sound. Those lost in the land of Ashur will come, also those scattered through the land of Egypt; and they will worship Adonai on the holy mountain in Yerushalayim" (Isaiah 27:13, CJB).

Notice the phrase that Yeshua uses to explain who knows when He will return: "But when that day and hour will come, no-one knows - not the angels in heaven, nor the Son, only the Father" (Matthew 24:26, CJB). Judaism uses a lunar calendar, with, in biblical times, each month being proclaimed by the *Sanhedrin* in Jerusalem after receiving the reliable testimony of two witnesses who have seen the new moon. All the other feasts in the Jewish calendar are at least a week into the month, thus allowing time for messengers to get to each community from Jerusalem. *Yom Teruah* alone is on the first day of the month bringing with it a high degree of uncertainty as to exactly when the feast would be; you could count the days of the previous month so that you had an approximate idea, but hence the saying about *Yom Teruah*: "no-one knows the day or the hour".

Further Study: Nehemiah 1:4-11; 1 Thessalonians 5:1-6

Application: Are you ready for or anticipating the Lord's return at any day? The physical blasts of the *shofar* are a powerful wake-up call - have you heard them recently? Do you remember their message of challenge and anticipation? How can you prepare for the High Holy Days and be ready for Yeshua's possible return?

Emor - Say - 6

Vayikra / Leviticus 23:33 - 44

Vayikra/Leviticus 23:35 On the first day, a holy convocation ...

בַּיוֹם הָרִאשׁוֹן מִקְרָא־קֹדֶשׁ
kodesh   mikra   ha'rishon   bayom

There is some discussion between the commentators as to whether the word מִקְרָא here should be מִקְרָה. Although BHS[7] shows no textual variants at this point, some commentators would prefer to see the latter over the former. מִקְרָא is derived from the root קָרָא - to call out, cry, shout, invoke - in one of the more common ways of constructing Hebrew nouns: adding a מ before the first root letter, which most often produces a noun describing either the place where the verb action takes place or the tool used to perform that action[8]. This noun has the sense of "a place of calling" and is translated by various bibles as a convocation or assembly. In the same way, מִקְרָה is derived from the root קָרָה - to meet or to happen - and has the sense of "a place of meeting or happening" and is translated as an event or result.

Although מִקְרָא is unambiguously used in this verse in a construct with the following word, giving the literal translation "a convocation of holiness", Rashbam prefers to read it as if it were מִקְרָה and writes, "whenever the word spelt with an *alef* is used in relation to a holiday it denotes an event, as if spelt with a *hay*. This is how the word is translated in *Targum Onkelos* and *Targum Jonathan*."

The idea of the feast days being events leads to the rabbinic view that they should be turned from just a holiday into specific times of holiness, meetings between man and *HaShem* through the setting apart of the day. Nachmanides, for example, instructs that "all the people should come

---

7. Biblia Hebraica Stuttgartensia - see Bibliography

8. For example: the root זָבַח - to sacrifice - and its noun מִזְבֵּחַ - an altar, or the root פָּתַח - to open - and its noun מַפְתֵּחַ - a key

together on that day and be assembled to sanctify it, for it is a commandment upon Israel to be gathered together in God's house on the festival day to hallow it publicly with prayer and praise to God, and with clean garments, and to make it a day of feasting as it is said in the tradition, 'Go, eat of the fat, drink of the sweet, and send portions to him who has nothing prepared; for this day is holy to our Lord. Do not be grieved, for the joy of the Lord is your strength' (Nehemiah 8:10, NASB)". This is how we are make to the days special. He goes on, "As our rabbis of blessed memory have said: 'Proclaim them with food and drink and clean garments' (Sifre, Pinchas 147); that is to say, the nature of these days should not be to you like that of other days, but instead you should make them occasions of holiness, changing them by food and dress from the common to the holy." This custom is still seen in Judaism today where people will buy or make new clothes for the holidays or give a gift of material from which new clothes can be made.

Rashi, whose translators prefer "a calling of holiness", points out: "Sanctify it with clean clothing and with prayer". This is a reference to the Talmud where the Sages say: "Where is the blessing of the sanctification of the day to be said? It has been taught: Rabbi[9] says, It should be said with the kingship verses. For just as on every other occasion we find that it comes fourth [in the order of blessings], so here it should come fourth." (*b.* Rosh Hashana 32*a*). This means that a special blessing for each festival day is said as the fourth benediction in the shortened *Amidah* prayer said as part of all the services which take place in that day. So not only is the day sanctified by food, drink and clean or new clothing, but it is also recognised by a special blessing in the main prayer that is considered to be the replacement for the sacrifices.

The Gospels record events when Yeshua took part in celebrations. The first instance seems to be the wedding at Cana in the Galil. John records that Yeshua's mother had been invited and "Yeshua too was invited to the wedding, along with his talmidim" (John 2:2, CJB). When the wine ran out, Yeshua - however reluctantly, at his mother's urging - miraculously replenished the supply of wine from jars of water. Yeshua recognised the importance of celebrations and life-cycle events and so performed a miracle to stop this particular one being washed out due to a shortage of wine. Similarly Luke recorded that "On their way Yeshua and His talmidim came to a village where a woman named Marta welcomed him into her home. She had a sister called Miryam who also sat at the Lord's feet and heard what he had to say. But Marta was busy with all the work to be done" (Luke 10:38-40, CJB). If Yeshua and the disciples were to spend time, celebrate and share His

9. When the title 'Rabbi' appears in the rabbinic writings alone, with no other name, it refers to Rabbi Judah ha Nasi, Rabbi Judah the Prince, the codifier of the *Mishnah*

teaching, then a festive meal was an essential part of that process; Martha should do enough, but not be worried about every last detail. On the other hand, when Yeshua entered Jerusalem a few days before *Pesach*, "Yeshua entered the Temple grounds and drove out those who were doing business there, both the merchants and their customers. He upset the desks of the money-changers and knocked over the benches of those who were selling pigeons" (Matthew 21:12, CJB). Although the dishonesty of the traders and the very existence of trade in God's house was offensive, the unabated continuation of every-day activities during the approach of the feast would distract people from the holiness of the pilgrimage they had made to appear before God. Yeshua wanted the people to use and enjoy appropriate celebrations and times of holiness, without the detraction of every day work and commercial activity.

In a different context, Rav Sha'ul rebukes the community in Corinth about their behaviour at their memorial meals to remember Yeshua: "as you eat your meal, each one goes ahead on his own; so that one stays hungry while another is already drunk!" (1 Corinthians 11:21, CJB). "What are you doing," Sha'ul wants to know, "don't you have homes to eat and drink in?" (v. 22, CJB). Remembering Yeshua is a holy moment, a time when the body of Messiah gathers to remember Him together and declare their faith in what He has done for us. Sha'ul points out that "whoever eats the Lord's bread or drinks the Lord's cup in an unworthy manner will be guilty of desecrating the body and blood of the Lord!" (v. 27, CJB) and urges the believers to examine themselves and moderate their conduct. Although this passage is often used to teach repentance of sin before sharing communion, the plain meaning of the text is at least as much about courtesy and table manners. Sha'ul again: "So then, my brothers, when you gather together to eat, wait for one another. If someone is hungry, he should eat at home, so that when you meet together it will not result in judgment" (vv. 33-34, CJB). The whole passage is all too frequently used as justification for great solemnity, absolute silence and an atmosphere rather more akin to a funeral than a celebration. Sharing at the Lord's Table is a moment of victory and triumph when we each remember and savour what Yeshua accomplished for us at Calvary; there should be shouts of praise, perhaps a few tears, shy grins, rejoicing laughter, sighs of relaxation and an almost euphoric air of freedom and liberty. We have been set free from the curse of sin and death and Yeshua has risen from the grave!

How do we celebrate the feasts today, from *Shabbat* each week to the highest of the feasts and Holy days? Do we set the day apart with special food, eaten only on these days to mark the days as holy? Do we refrain from going shopping after services, not only to obey the commands but to avoid every-day mundane commercial activity on a holy day? Do we wear different - not necessarily smart or fancy, although that might help, but at least clean - clothes to differentiate from our usual uniforms[10] on the feasts? Our text challenges us to have a day of "holy calling apart" on the feasts; time set apart for God when, as we have fun and celebrate, we also remember who He is, what He has done and our relationship with Him.

Further Study: 2 Chronicles 30:21-23; Luke 15:21-24

Application: Are you able to celebrate holy days and times before God and with His people, or do you always have half an eye on all the stuff that is waiting to be done? Why not ask God to show you how to set aside every-day concerns and enter into holy time so you can rejoice and celebrate Him!

---

10. Even a business suit can be a uniform if we wear it for work every other day of the week!

Emor - Say - 7

Vayikra / Leviticus 24:1 - 23

Vayikra/Leviticus 24:2 ... oil of the olive, clear, crushed for the light, to bring up a light continually.

שֶׁמֶן זַיִת זָךְ כָּתִית לַמָּאוֹר לְהַעֲלֹת נֵר תָּמִיד:
tamiyd   neyr   l'ha'alot   lama'or   katiyt   zach zayit shemen

The Hebrew text includes a number of unusual words. The adjective זָךְ comes from the root זָכַךְ - to be clean, clear and pure, both physically and morally - the verb is used in the *Hif'il* stem to mean "to cleanse": "If I should wash myself with snow and <u>cleanse</u> my hands with lye" (Job 9:30, NASB, emphasis added). The adjective כָּתִית comes from the root כָּתַת - to pulverise, crush or grind - here it is passive and is often translated "beaten"; the verb is also used in an active way: "And they will <u>hammer</u> their swords into ploughshares, and their spears into pruning hooks" (Isaiah 2:4, NASB, emphasis added) and "He also <u>broke into pieces</u> the bronze serpent that Moses had made" (2 Kings 18:4, NASB, emphasis added). These words are being used here in a technical sense, describing the way that olives are processed to produce the oil. The olives are broken up into pieces without being liquidised or mashed into an unrecognisable pulp.

In the years after the destruction of the Second Temple, the early rabbis recorded many of the ritual practices so that they could be re-instated when the Temple - as they then anticipated - was rebuilt. There is a lengthy description of the olive preparation process in the Mishnah (*m.* Menachot 8:4-5) which helps us to understand how the biblical words implemented:

> There are three [periods of gathering in the] olives and each crop gives three kinds of oil. The first crop of olives is when the olives are picked from the top of the tree; they are pounded [in a mortar] and put into the basket [and the oil oozes out and filters through the basket into the vessel below]; this gives the first oil. Then they are pressed with the beam (R. Judah says, with stone [weights]); this gives the

second oil. They are finally ground and pressed again; this gives the third oil. The first [oil] is fit for the Menorah and the others for meal-offerings. The second crop is when the olives at roof-level are picked from the tree [and processed in the same way]. The third crop is when the last olives [so low down that they will never ripen on the tree] of the tree are packed in the vat until they become overripe [lit. become rotten]; they are then taken up and dried on the roof and then pounded and [processed in the same way].

As to the first oil of the first crop, there is none better than it. The second oil of the first crop and the first oil of the second crop are equal. The third oil of the first crop, the second oil of the second crop and the first oil of the third crop are equal. The third oil of the second crop and the second oil of the third crop are equal. As to the third oil of the third crop, there is none worse than it.

Only the first oil was suitable for use in the *menorah*; that extracted with the minimum of processing and coercion. The first pressing was for the Lord; the subsequent pressings were for commercial use. There is a similar classification of olive oil in the Italian and Greek oil producing families today with the first "cold pressed", "virgin" oil being highly prized and valued, sometimes never let out of the family onto the market. In this picture, we can see the way that the oil to be used in the *menorah* was prized and valued by *HaShem* - only the best, willingly and carefully given, was appropriate for use in the Sanctuary.

Yeshua told a parable about a man who had two sons: "He went to the first and said, 'Son, go and work today in the vineyard.' He answered, 'I don't want to'; but later he changed his mind and went. The father went to his other son and said the same thing. This one answered, 'I will, sir'; but he didn't go" (Matthew 21:28-30, CJB). He then asked the Chief Priests and elders what they thought: "'Which of the two did what his father wanted?' 'The first,' they replied" (v. 31, CJB); what else could they say! Although he initially refused to go and work, he then did go; the second said that he would but didn't follow that up with action. "'That's right!' Yeshua said to them. 'I tell you that the tax-collectors and prostitutes are going into the Kingdom of God ahead of you! For Yochanan came to you showing the path to righteousness, and you wouldn't trust him. The tax-collectors and prostitutes trusted him; but you, even after you saw this, didn't change your minds later and trust him'" (vv. 31-32, CJB). The Chief Priests and elders were needing a lot of processing, a lot of squeezing to get them to make any movement, so although they made the right noises, nothing was happening - they didn't turn up for work. The tax-collectors and prostitutes, and those who were looked down as being "sinners" because they didn't keep up to the high standards of the religious professionals, might have initially appeared to be ignoring God's invitation to enter the kingdom, but by their actions they were now demonstrating that they didn't need any processing or squeezing - they were only too ready to accept God's invitation.

We can see this reflected again in the account of the olive processing above. The "first" pressing from all three grades - even though they were collected at different times, from olives of widely differing quality and ripeness - was considered suitable for use in the *menorah*. It was the amount of processing that made the difference; if the olive mass had to be re-ground or explicit mechanical pressure exerted to extract the oil, then although it could be used for meal offerings - which were largely consumed by the priests - it was not suitable for burning in the *menorah* as a total offering (like the burnt offering, which had to be without blemish) to the LORD.

So it is with us. Whether young or old, whether our first religious experience or the last of many as we trawled through this, that and the other on the way to really hearing about the kingdom, God is interested in whether we accepted His offer willingly and followed up with our actions, or whether we were strong-armed into it, gave a reluctant verbal but not heart commitment, and then did nothing about it. Many people have a few false starts before finding Yeshua; some resist Him for years until they really hear what it is all about, but then they can't wait to sign up and God's grace for them simply shines through their lives as they are turned completely around.

Yeshua never asked the first disciples to make converts; He asked them to make more disciples. He wasn't - and still isn't - after yes-men who say the words but do nothing, who have a Bible on their bookshelf but never read it, who put money into the collection when the bag goes round but never give sacrificially and unseen to the poor and needy on their doorstep. Rav Sha'ul told the Corinthians that "God loves a cheerful giver" (2 Corinthians 9:7); this is much less about money than about the way that time, resources, hospitality, good-cheer, companionship and life are given: in an open-handed way, freely and willingly rather than grudgingly and belatedly after much coercion and squeezing. That is the offering that is suitable for burning in the *menorah*, that makes the light in the Sanctuary dance and glow even when it is dark outside.

Further Study: 2 Chronicles 13:8-12; Matthew 20:4-7; 1 Corinthians 15:58

Application: A is for Attitude. Do we always get an 'A' for our attitude towards God and obeying Him willingly when He asks us to do or give something? What kind of offering do we bring - is it the first pressing or the hard squeeze?

בְּהַר/בְּחֻקֹּתַי

B'har/B'hukkotai - On mountain/In my regulations

Vayikra / Leviticus 25:1 - 27:34

- in leap years, the two *parashiyot* are read separately; in regular years, they are read together -

רִאשׁוֹן	Aliyah One	Vayikra/Leviticus 25:1 - 18
שְׁלִישִׁי	Aliyah Three	Vayikra/Leviticus 25:29 - 38
רְבִיעִי	Aliyah Four	Vayikra/Leviticus 25:39 - 26:9
שִׁשִּׁי	Aliyah Six	Vayikra/Leviticus 27:1 - 15
שְׁבִיעִי	Aliyah Seven	Vayikra/Leviticus 27:16 - 34

The text for Aliyah Six in this *parasha* is out of sequence.

בְּהַר - Vayikra/Leviticus 25:1 - 26:2

| שֵׁנִי | Aliyah Two | Vayikra/Leviticus 25:14 - 18 |
| חֲמִשִׁי | Aliyah Five | Vayikra/Leviticus 25:29 - 38 |

בְּחֻקֹּתַי - Vayikra/Leviticus 26:3 - 27:34

| שֵׁנִי | Aliyah Two | Vayikra/Leviticus 26:6 - 9 |
| חֲמִשִׁי | Aliyah Five | Vayikra/Leviticus 27:16 - 21 |

בְּהַר/בְּחֻקֹּתַי א׳

B'har/B'hukkotai - On mountain/In my regulations - 1

(In a leap year this could be read as B'har 1)

Vayikra / Leviticus 25:1 - 18

Vayikra/Leviticus 25:1 And Adonai spoke to Moshe on Mt. Sinai

וַיְדַבֵּר יהוה אֶל־מֹשֶׁה בְּהַר סִינַי

Siynay   b'har   Moshe   el   Adonai vay'dibeyr

One of the foundational tenets of Orthodox Judaism is that both the Written and Oral *Torah* were given to Moshe at Mt. Sinai. Rashi makes the connection here at the start of this *parasha*, before a set of detailed laws dealing with the seven-year agricultural cycle, that even these specific instructions were given to Moshe here in the desert at Mt. Sinai. Rashi also makes the point that this particular set of laws is not repeated on the Plains of Moab in the book of D'varim, to demonstrate that all the *Torah*, whether repeated elsewhere or not, originates at Sinai (Torat Kohanim, *Sefer Zikaron*). Although Judaism naturally recognises the role that Moshe played during the departure from Egypt, his status as *Moshe Rabbeinu* (Moses our Teacher) comes from the revelation and teaching of the *Torah* at Mt. Sinai - everything before then fades by comparison to the start of his real ministry at this pivotal moment in our people's history.

It is surely no co-incidence that we find Yeshua, almost at the start of His ministry, gathering His disciples around Him above the crowds, up a hill by the Sea of Galilee, to give one of the longest single discourses recorded in the gospels, known as the Sermon on the Mount (Matthew 5-7). In a wide ranging survey of *Torah* and the way it was being taught by the rabbis of His time, Yeshua focuses on the key functions and purposes to correct some of the misinterpretations that had developed over time. In fact, He was working in exactly the same way as Moshe, as an *halachic* authority, making rulings as to how *Torah* should be applied and worked out in everyday life. Unlike the rabbis, however, Yeshua taught with authority so that the account finishes with the comment: "When Yeshua had finished saying these things, the crowds were amazed at the way He taught, for He was not instructing them like their Torah-teachers but as one who had authority Himself" (Matthew 7:28-29, CJB).

A lot of things in this world depend on authority: how much you have and where you got it from. In business, levels of expenditure and authority are decided by the Board or senior management; in the academic world, your position is determined by your degree and university, then the number of papers you have had published. So it isn't surprising to find that Scripture comments on the authority of Moshe and Yeshua. The *Torah* quotes God Himself as saying, "Moshe is the only one faithful in My entire household" (B'Midbar 12:7, CJB). But the book of Hebrews, building on that passage from the *Torah* adds, "But Yeshua deserves more honour than Moshe, just as the builder of the house deserves more honour than the house ... Moshe was faithful in all God's house, as a servant giving witness to things that God would divulge later. But the Messiah, as Son, was faithful over God's house" (Hebrews 3:3-6, CJB).

Further Study: 1 Samuel 2:35-36; Matthew 25:14-23

Application: It is easy, when becoming involved in studying Judaism to learn the ways and traditions of our people, to lose sight of the difference between Moshe and Yeshua. Today is a day to refocus and know that Yeshua is Messiah!

בְּהַר ב׳

B'har - On mountain - 2

(In an ordinary year this could be read as B'har/B'hukkotai 1)

Vayikra / Leviticus 25:14 - 18

Vayikra/Leviticus 25:14 And when you sell a sale to your neighbour or buy from the hand of your neighbour

וְכִי־תִמְכְּרוּ מִמְכָּר לַעֲמִיתֶךָ אוֹ קָנֹה מִיַּד
miyad kano o la'amitecha mim'kar tim'kiru v'chiy

עֲמִיתֶךָ
amiytecha

The word עֲמִית, neighbour or society-member, is closely related to עַם, people. Whilst the latter is used to refer to whole people groups - יִשְׂרָאֵל עַמִּי, 'Israel My people', and the other peoples with whom Israel comes into contact, as opposed to גּוֹיִם, nations, which is used for the nations in a corporate sense - עֲמִית is used in a much more local or parochial sense: society, neighbour, community. Rashi comments that while the verse - enjoining honesty and fair pricing in business transactions - has a clear 'plain' meaning reading, the exegetical interpretation is that Jews should primarily trade with each other in preference to non-Jews. The super-commentaries pick up on the fact that the text talks about both buying and selling with one's neighbours which has a degree of redundancy about it, to emphasise that one should buy from and sell to fellow Jews (Torat Kohanim).

Over the years, the practical meaning of 'neighbour' changed. In Avraham's time, it would have meant the community that travelled with him - his household: family, servants, slaves and so on. By the times of the walled cities in the days of the kings, it would have referred to your physical neighbours in the city, be they Jew or *Ger* (alien living in the Land). After the division into the two kingdoms, the two exiles and the return to the Land, there was a definite separation between Judea and Galilee; by Second Temple times, this was quite marked, with Jews from the Galil having their lineage as Jews questioned by those who lived in Judea, and being regarded as second-class citizens of Israel. Forced re-settlement by the Assyrians had brought other peoples into the Land who although not of direct Jewish ancestry adopted many of the religious practices of the Land and inter-married with the people left behind - they became known as the Samaritans.

Against that background, we find Yeshua being asked quite a politically charged question: "And who is my neighbour?" (Luke 10:29, NASB). Although the text here suggests that the questioner asked that in order to justify himself, there is also every possibility that the enquiry was both serious and in earnest: in the light of all the peoples around, where are the boundaries of עֲמִית? Just who is my community?

In response, Yeshua tells the parable of the Good Samaritan with its surprise ending. The listeners would have been paying careful attention as Yeshua spoke, probably laughing at His caricature of the Priest and the Levite, but the ending would have shocked them. The Samaritans were a despised - and sometimes hated - minority, with travellers going out of their way to avoid passing through Samaria on their way between Judea and the Galil; but it was the Samaritan who crossed the boundary of hostility in order to demonstrate compassion to a Jew and show who God had in mind when He talked about neighbours.

Further Study: Luke 10:25-37

Application: Look around you today, at work and at the shops - do you see your neighbour there among the people? Buy and sell with your neighbour; interact with the community. As Yeshua said, "Go and do likewise" (Luke 10:37 CJB).

בְּהַר / בְּחֻקֹּתַי ג׳

B'har/B'hukkotai - On mountain/In my regulations - 3

(In a leap year this could be read as B'har 5)

Vayikra / Leviticus 25:29 - 38

Vayikra/Leviticus 25:29 And if a man will sell a dwelling house of a walled city

וְאִישׁ כִּי־יִמְכֹּר בֵּית־מוֹשַׁב עִיר חוֹמָה

khomah   iyr   moshav beyt   yim'kor kiy   v'iysh

The Talmud records some debate (*b.* Arachin 36*b*) over the exact status of the house and the walled city: the legal status of the house for redemption of a sale depends on the city - was it originally enclosed or surrounded later, and when the city was built. The consensus opinion is that the phrase "walled city" refers only to those cities which were enclosed in walls at the time of the conquest and were taken by Joshua and the men of Israel when they took possession of the Land after the Exodus from Egypt. Then, a house in the city is easily defined as one that is built within the city walls, rather than being built first outside and later enclosed by the walls of a city that grew around the houses.

Throughout history, but particularly in modern times when there is so much housing development, there has been the phenomenon of urban sprawl, or perhaps more correctly, urban creep. Areas that were originally outside a city gradually become enclosed as the pressure for housing (and the desire to 'escape' the confines of city life) leads to the building of new homes on agricultural land and not only the physical city expands, but the influence and control of the city spreads through the economic need to provide food and other resources for the consumers in the (growing) city. It is odd to look back and think that in the 15th century, Fleet Street - now in the heart of London - was simply farmland beside the Fleet River, and that Moorfields - as the name suggests - was a set of fields immediately outside the city wall on the north used for grazing cattle, that often flooded in winter, and was used by the apprentices from the city of London for playing ball games on the afternoons of the church holy days.

Creep or spread of influence from a city or stronghold into the surrounding area is not limited to physical towns and cities. The same phenomenon can be seen at work in the spiritual world, where the powers of darkness and evil seek to control and dominate by a gradual process of extension from their power-bases of wickedness. The gradual but inexorable erosion of the freedom to preach the Gospel and witness openly for God in the face of tolerance, pluralism and political correctness is only the prelude to lifestyles that are sinking into immorality, breakdown of marriage, hopelessness, insanity and organised crime.

But that isn't the way God sees it. Just as a house outside a city could always be redeemed (cf. verse 31), so God can always redeem those who turn to Him. Yeshua said, "I will build My community and the gates of Sh'ol will not overcome it" (Matthew 16:18, CJB). The kingdom of God will not be affected by urban sprawl from the strongholds of the enemy; on the contrary, "for the weapons of our warfare are not of the flesh, but divinely powerful for the destruction of fortresses" (2 Corinthians 10:4, NASB). God's perspective is that we are the ones who are taking ground!

Further Study: Ephesians 6:10-18; Isaiah 12:6

Application: Are you embittered or embattled, hunkered down and waiting for the cavalry to come over the hill? Take a fresh look at things from God's perspective; don't believe the propaganda coming from the world. The time has come to take the offensive!

בְּהַר 'ה

B'har - On mountain - 5

(In an ordinary year this could be read as B'har/B'hukkotai 3)

Vayikra / Leviticus 25:29 - 38

Vayikra/Leviticus 25:31 And the houses of the open space, that have no walls around them

וּבָתֵּי הַחֲצֵרִים אֲשֶׁר אֵין־לָהֶם חֹמָה סָבִיב
saviyv khomah lahem eyn asher hakhatzeriym oovatey

The word הֶחֲצֵרִים comes from a root חָצַר that is not used in biblical Hebrew; its Arabic equivalent means "to enclose" or "to call together". The noun חָצֵר is listed by Davidson as meaning "an enclosure, area, court" or "village, hamlet"; the second meaning seems more likely in the context of this verse. *Targum Onkelos* chooses the word פַּצְחַיָּא, meaning "open" or "unwalled", the same choice as in B'resheet 25:16 and D'varim 3:5 and that *Targum Jonathan* gives in Joshua 13:28, seeming to follow the simple meaning of the text. Rashi also supports this: "the houses of the yards: open towns without a wall"; he also quotes Joshua 13:28 "the walled cities and their open towns" and B'resheet 25:16, "in their open towns and in their cities".

Baruch Levine comments on the history of the word. While D'varim 2:23 relates that the land of the Ammonites was once populated by a people who lived in "tents", and Isaiah 42:11 describes the Kedemite tribes living in tents encampments near Petra, in the genealogy of Ishmael given in B'resheet 25:12 ff., the clans live in "circular encampments". In this text, however, the scene has changed from a nomadic lifestyle to a more fixed or settled pattern. Levine says, "Here, reference is primarily to agricultural villages, where there were houses, not tents, and fields, not pastureland." This then is part of the contrast between houses built within walled cities, or within their curtilage, and houses that are part of agricultural settlements, built among the among the fields without protecting walls.

The surrounding verses are discussing the conveyance and redemption rules for houses and land, particularly in the context of the jubilee year. "If someone sells a dwelling in walled city, he has one year after the date of sale in which to redeem it ... but if he has not redeemed the dwelling in the walled city within the year, then title in perpetuity passes to the buyer through all his generations; it will not revert in the yovel[ll]. However, houses in villages not surrounded by walls are to be dealt with like the fields of the countryside - they may be redeemed, and they revert in the yovel" (Vayikra 25:29-31, CJB). A house that is in a city, an enclosed space, only has a short time window for redemption - to be bought back if the seller changes his mind or comes into the financial means - otherwise the sale becomes permanent, even enduring the year of Jubilee. A house that is out in the countryside, on the other hand, is treated like the fields in which it is located: it is part of someone's livelihood, part of the means of making an income, so may always be redeemed and reverts to its original owner in the year of Jubilee. The right of redemption meant that even after an item had been sold - be that land, a house or even a person - the original owner or his family (tribe, clan, extended family) could insist upon the reversal of the sale and the transfer back to the owner of the item concerned, provided that they could pay the value of the item at that time. The purchaser could, of course, use the item in the meantime, but had no choice but to surrender it if a person with the right of redemption produced the money and demanded that it be so. In the year of Jubilee, all non-permanent conveyances of land and property reverted to their original owners without any money changing hands. Therefore, the maximum time that a field, for example, could be "out" of a family's ancestral holdings was between one Jubilee year and the next: 50 years. The price of an item was therefore governed by the number of years that a purchaser had until the Jubilee, the number of crops or crop-cycles that could be worked from the soil in that time.

The essential difference between open and closed territory is that the open can always be redeemed, whereas the closed is transferred in perpetuity after a short time window when it can be redeemed. This is an interesting picture of our lives and the way we are affected by sin. Sin closes us down, so that we become unavailable to our original owner for "the wages of sin is death" (Romans 6:23). We have only a short window in which to try and redeem the situation - have you noticed that the longer you wait to say 'sorry' for offending someone, the more difficult it becomes? One sin leads to another until we become completely trapped in habits of sin that seem impossible to break. Even those who have had relationship with God can be trapped in this way so that after a time they become just like all the people of the world around them. The sin builds a wall around the person so that instead of being a house in the open space, redeemable on demand, they become a dwelling in a walled city, transferred in perpetuity to another owner.

---

11. Jubilee year

How desperate this would be if it were not for another verse earlier in the chapter: God says, "The land is not to be sold in perpetuity, because the land belongs to Me - you are only foreigners and temporary residents in Me" (Vayikra 25:23, CJB). Although we may think that we hold the head lease, God remains the freeholder and can always exercise His right of redemption. Yeshua paid the price for our sin so that when we turn to Him, He demands our release from the current lease-holder and tears down the wall that sin has built around us, returning us to relationship with God and the open spaces where we can bring forth a crop of righteousness for Him.

Further Study: Psalm 49:7-8; Joel 2:18-20

Application: Where are you? Are you a house in the open space, with no walls around you, open to God and able to fellowship with Him, or are you closed in, surrounded by walls of sin, closed off and feeling that you have been sold in perpetuity? Turn to God today and ask Him to exercise His rights of freehold in Messiah Yeshua to redeem you and set you free.

בְּהַר/בְּחֻקֹּתַי ד'

B'har/B'hukkotai - On mountain/In my regulations - 4

(In a leap year this could be read as B'hukkotai 2)

Vayikra / Leviticus 25:39 - 26:9

Vayikra/Leviticus 25:39 And if your brother becomes impoverished with you and is sold to you ...

וְכִי־יָמוּךְ אָחִיךָ עִמָּךְ וְנִמְכַּר־לָךְ

lach v'nimkar imach akhiycha yamuch v'chiy

Baruch Levine points out that the whole of this section, verses 39-46, deal with indenture: "An Israelite indentured to another must not be treated as a slave." So the verb נִמְכַּר, a *Niphal* affix 3ms form of the root מָכַר, which has a range of meanings from "to sell, receive in marriage" to "to deliver or give into the power of another", should be understood as a legal indenture process. The poor man receives a capital sum for agreeing to be the indentured servant of another Israelite for a certain period of time, that he uses to settle his debts. The contract guarantees him food, clothing, shelter and a better standard of service and living than that which an owned slave would be entitled to enjoy.

Hirsch, on the other hand, starts by looking at the word עִמָּךְ, "with you", and draws attention to the degree of poverty involved: in spite of being assisted by his fellow Israelites, the man "still had not been able to save himself from financial ruin," so has sold himself as a last resort. Hirsch quotes the *halacha* that states that "selling oneself is only allowed under the pressure of the very extremist degree of dire necessity, where no other possibility opens itself to find the means of continuing existence."

Nechama Leibowitz sees this text as the third stage in a four-step process, starting in verse 25: "If your brother becomes poor, and has sold away some of his possessions"; then verse 35: "If your brother grows poor and his hand failed with you, then you shall strengthen him"; then this text, followed by verse 47: "If your brother sells himself to a stranger who has grown rich with you". At each stage, regardless of any direct family relationship, the poor man is described as "your brother", for all in Israel are a part of the commonwealth of Israel. The community is obliged to help the sufferer: firstly by redeeming his estate and home which he had been unable to maintain; secondly by extending interest-free loans loans to strengthen him; thirdly to take him as an indentured slave; and lastly that even if the community itself cannot assist him so that he sells himself to a rich Gentile, to ensure that the provisions of the Jubilee year are understood and obeyed by that Gentile.

Yeshua tells the parable of the Good Samaritan in Luke 10 to illustrate how this is to be worked out. Although the establishment figures declined to help the man who had been beaten and robbed - whether to avoid ritual impurity, for fear of their own personal security or simply because they didn't - he was helped by a Samaritan traveller. The Samaritans and the Jews did not see eye to eye on a range of issues, as a number of gospel passages make clear, yet out of common decency and compassion, it was a Samaritan who picked up and cared for the beaten and wounded Jewish man; more, he took him to an inn, paid for several days of food and care and underwrote his future costs until well enough to travel for himself. "Which of these three do you think proved to be a neighbour to the man who fell into the robbers' hands?" (Luke 10:36, NASB) Yeshua asked. This is so obvious - that compassion and mercy should call us to cross boundaries of race, colour and even creed - that we will sometimes miss it. Moreover, it is not to be done simply as an evangelistic tool, for that is essentially a selfish motive: helping others so that you can fulfill your own obligation to share the gospel! Instead, we are to extend mercy and compassion because it is the right thing to do, because it is what God does, because it is what Yeshua did. That is why Rav Sha'ul writes, "anyone who does not provide for his own people, especially for his family, has disowned the faith and is worse than an unbeliever" (1 Timothy 5:8, CJB) and our text sets this firmly in the heart of the believing community.

Further Study: Romans 12:9-13; Isaiah 58:6-7

Application: Do you see those around you who are impoverished or obviously struggling to make ends meet? Do you have the means to help them - by way of support, counsel or simply fellowship? Here is an opportunity to share God's mercy and compassion - without thought or hope of return - because that is what Yeshua would do and wants to do through you.

B'hukkotai - In my regulations - 2

(In an ordinary year this could be read as B'har/B'hukkotai 4)

Vayikra / Leviticus 26:6 - 9

Vayikra/Leviticus 26:6 I will give peace in the Land

וְנָתַתִּי שָׁלוֹם בָּאָרֶץ

ba'aretz   shalom   v'natatiy

It is interesting that this verse, which starts a section dealing with peace and security, is bracketed by verses promising God's provision of plenty in the Land. Rashi comments, "Perhaps you will say, 'Here is food and here is drink; [but] if there is no peace, there is nothing!' The verse says, after all this, 'I will make peace in the Land.' From here we see that peace is as weighty as everything else. And so it says, 'He makes peace and creates all!' (see below)". Peace is the filling in the sandwich between two slices of bread - that God promises to bring forth from the earth - and just as you cannot have a sandwich without the bread, you cannot eat the bread without a filling; without peace there is no opportunity to enjoy the good things that the Lord will provide in the Land.

The Sages have a discussion in the Talmud (*b.* Berachot 11*b*) connecting this verse with Isaiah 45:7, "Forming light and creating darkness; making peace and creating evil; I am Adonai who makes all these." The Rabbis are a little squeamish openly to ascribe the creation of evil to God, so where this verse is quoted in the first blessing before the Shema in the *Shacharit* prayer service it is paraphrased to עֹשֶׂה שָׁלוֹם וּבוֹרֵא אֶת־הַכֹּל, "makes peace and creates all/everything". 'Everything' includes 'evil', so this is a generalisation to avoid being specific.

Isaiah prophesied of Messiah, "For a son to us will be born ... and His name will be called ... שַׂר־שָׁלוֹם, Prince of Peace" (Isaiah 9:5). Rav Sha'ul explains how this works: "For He Himself is our peace, who made both groups into one, and broke down the barrier of the dividing wall ... that in Himself He might make the two into one new man, thus establishing peace" (Ephesians 2:15-16, NASB). Yeshua Himself is our peace because He makes peace.

Notice the difference in the Isaiah verse: "making peace and creating evil"; whereas evil is simply created - spoken into existence and there it is - peace has to be made; it requires a hands-on effort to make peace by a process of reconciliation. Yeshua did this for us: reconciling us to God and making peace not only between God and man but between Jew and Gentile.

Rav Sha'ul makes it plain that we are to be involved: "God, who through the Messiah has reconciled us to Himself and has given us the work of that reconciliation ... therefore we are ambassadors of the Messiah" (2 Corinthians 5:18,20 CJB). God has called us to be actively involved in making peace, not simply abstaining from fighting or conflict ourselves. But it all comes from God - as the *Kaddish* says: "He who makes peace in His heights, may He make peace upon us and upon all Israel. Now respond: Amen."

Further Study: Matthew 5:9; Hebrews 12:14; Romans 12:8

Application: In our zeal to put the world to rights and speak out about justice and righteousness, it is easy to forget that sinners are people too, just like us, and that we can often be harsh and un-peaceful. Today would be a good day to know peace with God for ourselves and to share it with others.

בְּחֻקֹּתַי 'ה

B'hukkotai - In my regulations - 5

(In an ordinary year this could be read as B'har/B'hukkotai 6)

Vayikra / Leviticus 27:16 - 21

Vayikra/Leviticus 27:16 And your valuation shall be by the portion of its seed: a homer of barley seed for fifty shekels of silver

וְהָיָה עֶרְכְּךָ לְפִי זַרְעוֹ זֶרַע חֹמֶר שְׂעֹרִים

s'oriym khomer zera zar'o l'fiy er'k'cha v'haya

בַּחֲמִשִּׁים שֶׁקֶל כָּסֶף:

kasef shekel bakhamishiym

Our starting point for this week is the comment made by Richard Elliott Friedman, "The value of the land is determined by how much seed one can plant in it." The NJPS translation of the first part of the text reads, "its assessment shall be in accordance with its seed requirements" and Baruch Levine comments that this was a common method of sizing plots of land in the ancient Middle East: by how much seed it required to sow it. The formula זֶרַע חֹמֶר means the area that can be sown with a homer of seed and the word חֹמֶר comes from חָמֹר, an ass or mule. Levine says that the homer is a dry measure, equal to the load of an ass, perhaps between 4 - 6 bushels.

Rashi digs a little deeper into the matter: "The valuation shall be according to its seedings - And not according to its worth [on the open market]. Both a good field and a bad field, the redemption of their sanctity is equal." The larger context of this text is in a discussion of how fields that are sold are priced and redeemed in relation to the Jubilee year. This particular verse is concerned with a field that is part of an Israelite's ancestral holding that is being dedicated to *HaShem*, which makes it different from a commercial transaction. If a field is sold, either for a particular number of years or, at the most, until the Jubilee, then its sale price is based upon the quality and location of the field, its drainage, fertility and other factors that affect the yield that the purchaser may expect to get out of the field in the time available, even allowing for the sabbatical years that may fall due in the sale period; everything depends on what you can get out of the field. Rashi is telling us that exactly the opposite is true for a field that is consecrated to *HaShem*: its valuation - whether a good field or a bad one - is based entirely on its area and that is determined by the amount of seed that is needed to sow the field; everything depends on what you put into the field. Even if the temple treasurers then sell the field on a commercial basis, its redemption value by the original owner remains the same, on an equal footing with every other field; the price for redemption is the same.

What does that tell us, then, about the redemption of people by and before God? We know that some of the offerings for sin, for cleansing and other ritual functions are scaled by the ability of the person to pay: "But if he cannot afford a lamb, then he shall bring to the Lord his guilt offering for that in which he has sinned, two turtle doves or two young pigeons" (Vayikra 5:7, NASB). Do the scaling rules apply to basic atonement or redemption? It would appear not: "Each one who is numbered in the census shall give this: half a shekel according to the shekel of the sanctuary ... the rich shall not give more, and the poor shall not give less, than the half shekel, when you give the Lord's offering to make atonement for your lives" (Shemot 30:13,15, ESV). There is a possibility that this pricing arrangement was older even than Moshe's day - Avraham's servant's first gift to Rivka, by token of a symbolic purchase of her to be Yitz'chak's wife, was "a gold ring weighing half a shekel" (B'resheet 24:22, ESV). The half shekel was given for the upkeep of the sanctuary and was collected in Yeshua's time: "When they came to Capernaum, the collectors of the half-shekel tax went up to Peter and said 'Does your master not pay the tax?'" (Matthew 17:24, ESV). After the destruction of the Second Temple, the Roman emperor Vespasian imposed an annual tax of two drachmas to be paid by every Jew in the Roman empire to be used for the upkeep of the temple to Jupiter Capitolinus in Rome. This tax was still being collected in the third century as a punishment for the 1st Jewish Revolt in 66-70 CE (Cassius Dio 66.7.2, see Goodman page 581).

There are two outstanding claims to be the worst sinner: one by Rav Sha'ul: "It is a trustworthy statement, deserving full acceptance, that Messiah Yeshua came into the world to save sinners, among whom I am the foremost" (1 Timothy 1:15, NASB); the other by John Newton in his famous hymn: "Amazing grace, how sweet the sound, that saved a wretch like me". In both cases, the price of redemption was exactly the same: more than they could ever afford and yet free for the asking. Yeshua's death at the crucifixion stake paid the judicial price for sin for all those who acknowledge Him as Saviour and Lord as it says, "there is no difference between Jew and Gentile - Adonai is the same for everyone, rich towards everyone who calls on Him, since everyone who calls in the name of Adonai will be delivered" (Romans 10:12-13, CJB). God isn't concerned by what He can get out of us, since just like fields, some of us are well-drained and some of us are not; He is concerned by what He puts into us: His Son, "who gave Himself as a ransom on behalf of all" (1 Timothy 2:6, CJB). God has provided that ransom for each of us - every man, woman and child who will turn to Him - so that we who could never afford the penalty for sin might be free of the law of sin and death and live for righteousness in Him!

Further Study: Acts 4:34-37; 1 Corinthians 15:9-10; Ephesians 3:7-8

Application: Do you worry that you are not good enough for God? That He can't have saved you because you just aren't worth it? God values each of us exactly the same and wants to redeem everyone who will turn to Him. Whether a bad or a light sinner, we all need a saviour and He will be that for you if you ask Him. What are you waiting for?

בְּהַר/בְּחֻקֹּתַי ו׳

B'har/B'hukkotai - On mountain/In my regulations - 6

(In a leap year this could be read as B'hukkotai 6)

Vayikra / Leviticus 27:1 - 15

Vayikra/Leviticus 27:25 And every valuation shall be in the shekel of the sanctuary;

וְכָל־עֶרְכְּךָ יִהְיֶה בְּשֶׁקֶל הַקֹּדֶשׁ
hakodesh b'shekel yih'yeh er'k'cha v'chol

This verse comes in the middle of a discussion concerning the valuation of fields in particular, but other items as well, that have been dedicated to *Adonai*. Two types of financial transaction may follow from such a dedication and a time period is also involved: the Jubilee year when the field would revert to its ancestral owner or family. The priests were not, essentially, farmers and would not want to farm a field - particularly one that might be remote from Jerusalem or any of the cities where priests would live - for years until the Jubilee in order to bring the crops from that field into the Temple treasury, or undertake the sale of the crops to release their monetary value. The donated field was therefore made available for sale; the priestly treasury could sell the field to an arbitrary third party, who would then farm it until the Jubilee, for a sum representing the value of the crops that could be expected over that period, discounted to represent the forward investment. Alternatively, the field could be redeemed by its ancestral owner or family, who might not have been the person who donated it to *Adonai*; again, a valuation method is given which differs slightly from the 'sale' value because it is their own field.

In all cases, however, the *Torah* stipulates that the valuation must be made in sanctuary shekels and the text goes on to quantify exactly what a "sanctuary shekel" means in terms of another unit of measure, the *gerah*. This tells us three important things about the valuation. Firstly, the valuation must be made in precise monetary terms, not by comparison to the yields of other fields or the value of other types of asset; the valuation must be explicitly quantified so that everything is transparent and above board and could, if necessary, be challenged. In the case of the redemption valuation, there is a precise formula involved based on the area of the field, the average yield per unit area and the number of years until the year of Jubilee. Secondly, the valuation must be in a universally accepted unit, the shekel used in the sanctuary and maintained by the priests and Levites; therefore assumed to be strictly honest and consistent. Thirdly, the valuation is made in hard currency; the unit is not subject to variation, inflation, re-valuation or fluctuation, and is always backed by the resources of the Temple and thus by God Himself.

Through this passage and its parallels, the *Torah* teaches that everything has a value and that whether for sale, for offering to God or for redemption purposes, that value can be calculated. More, since these particular valuations - and other passages that allow different size or value offerings to be made either by people who can afford them or by the poor - are intricately involved in people's relationship with God, it teaches that God also values each person and that each person is unique and has a known and specific value to God. Ultimately, when talking about atonement, the *Torah* explains that only blood has the power of atonement: "For the life of the flesh is in the blood, and I have given it to you on the altar to make atonement for your souls; for it is the blood by reason of the life that makes atonement" (Vayikra 17:11, NASB). The ultimate value of life is a life; this is why a murderer is to be killed: not only as a punishment but because a life demands a life.

Matthew and Luke both record Yeshua teaching his *talmidim* about the value God places on human life, particularly in the face of opposition or persecution. Sandwiched between important promises about the secrets of those who would oppose the gospel being brought out into the open and Yeshua acknowledging before the Father those who acknowledge Him before men, we find this text: "Aren't sparrows sold for next to nothing, five for two assarions? And not one of them has been forgotten by God. Why, every hair on your head has been counted! Don't be afraid, you are worth more than many sparrows" (Luke 12:6-7, CJB). Even apparently insignificant little birds such as sparrows, that were sold in the markets for very small sums of money, had a value. They are valued individually by God who considers their lives important; the Matthew text says, "Yet not one of them will fall to the ground without your Father's consent" (Matthew 10:29, CJB) to emphasise that God numbers even the days of sparrows and that none die without His permission. So, Yeshua continues, you, His disciples then, we, His disciples now, have a value much greater than sparrows to God so that even the hairs on our heads (between 90,000-140,000 per person) are numbered and known to Him.

The same rules for valuation that are found in the *Torah* apply equally to our relationships with God. God values each one of us, saint or sinner, "for it is not His purpose that anyone should be destroyed, but that everyone should turn from his sins" (2 Peter 3:9, CJB). It is to this end - that we should come to know Him - that God Himself initiated what Derek Prince referred to as the "Great Exchange". God offered hard currency: "For God so loved the world that He gave His only begotten Son so that whosoever should believe in Him should not perish but have everlasting life" (John 3:16); He paid the standard unit - life for life - "[He] gave Himself for us, that He might redeem us from every lawless deed and purify for Himself a people for His own possession, zealous for good deeds" (Titus 2:14, NASB); He offered a precise valuation: "He made Him who knew no sin to be sin on our behalf, that we might become the righteousness of God in Him" (2 Corinthians 5:21, NASB). Yeshua even signed and sealed the transaction with His own blood.

Whilst God's love for us and the value that He places on us cannot be taken as a licence to disregard His calling on our lives or His commandments that we should keep, it is important that we realise just how much God has done for us and how highly He values us. Be encouraged with this today and hold your head up as a valued and highly prized child of the King, a member of the Body of Messiah and citizen of the Kingdom of Heaven.

Further Study: Proverbs 16:11; Job 38:41; Romans 8:3-4

Application: Do you struggle with your self-worth in the kingdom? Do you sometimes find it hard to think that God really loved you enough to send Yeshua to die on the cross for you? Do you worry that you're only here by mistake or even that you shouldn't really be here at all? If so, then this is for you. Every person has a precise and known value to God, each individual is unique and special, everybody matters to Him. The Great Exchange happened for you!

בְּהַר/בְּחֻקֹּתַי ז'

B'har/B'hukkotai - On mountain/In my regulations - 7

(In a leap year this could be read as B'hukkotai 7)

Vayikra / Leviticus 27:16 - 34

Vayikra/Leviticus 27:29 Any proscribed person, who has been proscribed from mankind, he shall not be redeemed - he shall certainly be put to death.

כָּל־חֵרֶם אֲשֶׁר יָחֳרַם מִן־הָאָדָם לֹא יִפָּדֶה

yipadeh lo ha'adam min yakharam asher kheyrem kol

מוֹת יוּמָת:

yumat mot

Coming at the conclusion of a passage dealing with items which have been dedicated - as offerings - to God in various ways, and whether they can or cannot be redeemed once so dedicated, this verse seems a startling change of topic. The verb חָרַם means to place under a ban or to commit to *HaShem* by total destruction. For example, the penalty of being placed under the ban is incurred for idolatry: "Whoever sacrifices to a god other than the Lord alone shall be proscribed" (Shemot 22:19, JPS). Used as a noun, חֵרֶם is here taken to mean a person who has been sentenced to death by due process of the courts. The text, then, says that once a person has been officially sentenced to execution, it is not possible for either himself or others to redeem him, either by the payment of a financial penalty or substitution of animal sacrifices. The Sages of the Mishnah and Talmud have a detailed discussion about this (cf. *b.* Arachin 6*b*) summarised by *Rashi*:

1. from the moment that the sentence has been passed, the process of death has begun and is irreversible
2. as a "dead man" the man has no value or worth; a redemption valuation cannot be made or paid

173

Taking a slightly different approach, Rabbi Samson Raphael Hirsch points out that unless the judge can be shown to have made a mistake, this is God's justice, against which there can be no appeal. Whilst human decisions - the subject of the previous verses - can be reversed or changed, even if at a cost, God never changes His mind, so He cannot be "bought off" from His justice. The *Torah* itself insists that once sentenced, the death penalty is immutable: "You may not accept a ransom for the life of a murderer who is guilty of a capital crime; he must be put to death" (B'Midbar 35:31, JPS).

The Scriptures tell us that Yeshua too was totally committed to God. In his vision of the apocalypse, John describes Yeshua as "the Lamb that was slain from the creation of the world" (Revelation 13:8, NIV). In other words, before time or creation itself began, Yeshua was already a dead man, awaiting the moment of execution. In that light, see how Isaiah describes him: "He had no form or beauty, that we should look at him: no charm, that we should find Him pleasing. He was despised, shunned by men, a man of suffering, familiar with disease. As one who hid his face from us, He was despised, we held Him of no account" (Isaiah 53:2-3, JPS). Isaiah prophesied that the leaders in Yeshua's time would place no value or worth upon Him, so that He could not be redeemed. Even when Pilate attempted to free Him, the crowd chose Barabbus - a condemned murderer - over Yeshua.

This was no accident, but the deliberate design of God; Peter explained to the people on the day of *Shavuot*, just seven weeks since Yeshua had been crucified and then resurrected again: "this Man, delivered up by the predetermined plan and foreknowledge of God, you nailed to a cross by the hands of godless men and put Him to death" (Acts 2:23, NASB). During His own ministry years with the disciples, Yeshua had made it plain to them what was going to happen to Him - "All these things Yeshua spoke to the multitudes in parables, and He did not speak to them without a parable, so that what was spoken through the prophet might be fulfilled, saying, 'I will open My mouth in parables; I will utter things hidden since the foundation of the world.'" (Matthew 13:34-35, NASB) - but they had almost as much difficulty as the crowd in understanding. After what many scholars take as a pivotal point in Yeshua's ministry - Peter's confession of Yeshua as Messiah at Caesarea Philippi - when Yeshua first spoke about His coming death, Peter went as far as to rebuke Him, "From that time on, Yeshua began making it clear to His talmidim that He had to go to Jerusalem and endure much suffering at the hands of the elders, the head cohanim and the Torah-teachers; and that He had to be put to death; but that on the third day, He had to be raised to life. Kefa took Him aside and began rebuking Him, 'Heaven be merciful, Lord! By no means will this happen to you!' 'You must not let this happen!', Peter urged. But Yeshua turned his back on Kefa, saying, 'Get behind Me, Satan! You are an obstacle in My path, because your thinking is from a human perspective, not from God's perspective!'" (Matthew 16:21-23, CJB). From the human perspective they had, the disciples thought that Yeshua had a choice; more, that God wouldn't allow Him to be killed. They couldn't see that the crucifixion and resurrection were already an accomplished action from God's eternal perspective; they just needed to happen within time.

Hebrew has a syntactic device used to express future actions that, although they haven't yet happened, are as good as done because in the writer's or character's mind they are certain; the decisions have already been taken. An example of this can be found in the book of Ruth. Boaz tells the kinsman redeemer that Naomi, Ruth's mother-in-law, has decided to sell the field that belonged to her late husband. Although the translations say, "Naomi is selling" (Ruth 4:3, NIV), "Naomi has to sell" (NASB), "Naomi must sell" (JPS), the Hebrew text has the word מָכְרָה, a plain *Qal* affix 3fs form. The affix form is most often translated in the past, as single event completed actions, but is here referring to a future event. This is known as an "affix of intent", meaning that the future event is so certain that to all intents and purposes it has already happened. The same device is being used prophetically in the Isaiah 53 quotation above, as Isaiah predicts the reaction of the Jewish leaders nearly six hundred years after his own lifetime.

Later in his life, Peter wrote to the early Jewish believers in Messiah scattered throughout the Roman world to confirm his certainty about the events that had happened in Jerusalem: "For He was foreknown before the foundation of the world, but has appeared in these last times for the sake of you" (1 Peter 1:20, NASB). Peter remains adamant that Yeshua's death was no accident, it was not a fall-back position as God switched from Plan A to Plan B because the Jewish leaders had rejected Yeshua. This had been God's plan all along, hidden from the world yet enigmatically hinted at throughout the Hebrew Scriptures. And the purpose? Why did He do all this? "For your sakes" (ibid., CJB). That's the simple truth: He did this for us.

Further Study: Isaiah 42:8-9; Matthew 24:36-37; Ephesians 1:11-12

Application: Do you share Peter's certainty about the plan and purpose of God? Know that the same certainty that governed Yeshua's life and ministry applies to God's plans for your life. "For I am mindful of the plans I have made concerning you -- declares the Lord -- plans for your welfare, not for disaster, to give you a hopeful future" (Jeremiah 29:11, JPS).

Pesach - Passover

Traditional "Festival Readings" are allocated for the different days of *Pesach*. Our readings are taken from both the traditional readings and other ancient sources.

רִאשׁוֹן	Day One	Shemot/Exodus 33:12
שֵׁנִי	Day Two	Shemot/Exodus 15:1
שְׁלִישִׁי	Day Three	Shemot/Exodus 12:3
רְבִיעִי	Day Four	Shemot/Exodus 12:29
חֲמִשִׁי	Day Five	Shemot/Exodus 13:17
שִׁשִׁי	Day Six	Shemot/Exodus 11:5
שְׁבִיעִי	Day Seven	Isaiah 60:2

פֶּסַח א'

Pesach - Passover - 1

Shemot/Exodus 33:12 Moshe said to HaShem, "Look, You say to me, 'Take this people onwards' ..."

וַיֹּאמֶר מֹשֶׁה אֶל־יהוה רְאֵה אַתָּה אֹמֵר אֵלַי
eylay omeyr atah r'eyh Adonai et Moshe vayomer

הַעַל אֶת־הָעָם הַזֶּה
ha'zeh ha'am et hayal

Both here and at the start of the story of our people leaving Egypt we appear to have a contradiction, at least in our understanding of God. There we read, "God heard their groaning, and God remembered His covenant with Avraham, Yitz'chak and Ya'akov. God saw the people of Israel, and God acknowledged them" (Shemot 2:24-25, CJB). Ignoring, for the moment, whether the anthropomorphisms of 'seeing' and 'hearing' are equivalent or appropriate to apply to God, both of these passages beg the question: Why is it necessary to draw God's attention to the situation, and why does the text give the impression that God only appeared to notice what was going on when He was forced to make a response? After all, the Scriptures tell us that "He who keeps Israel will neither slumber nor sleep" (Psalm 121:4, NASB) and, "He who touches Israel touches the apple of God's eye" (Zechariah 2:8).

These passages teach us an important aspect of God's character and our relationship with Him. Certainly God said, "before they call, I will answer" (Isaiah 65:24, NASB), but that pre-supposes that there is a call - the verse goes on, "while they are still speaking, I will hear". In other words, God's answer before we speak or ask depends on His foreknowledge that we are about to call on Him. If we are in relationship with God, then that relationship needs to be working and in functional order. Many people quote Rav Sha'ul's famous words to say, "God causes all things to work together for good" (Romans 8:28, NASB) forgetting the next phrase: "to those who love God ...". In other words, we have to have a working relationship with God and invite Him to be involved in our lives before those promises apply to us. Once we know God, it is also up to us to keep the channels of communication open, asking Him about things, involving Him in all the decisions we take in just the same way as we would our spouse.

So Moshe's "Look here" is part of an ongoing conversation and expresses as much his desire to talk about a particular subject as it does to focus God's attention on what Moshe wants to say. In the case of the Exodus narrative, our peoples' suffering in Egypt had reached the point where they wholeheartedly turned to God and stopped relying on their own strength and stamina - thus opening the way for God to act. This *Pesach* might be a good time to consider whether your channels of communication with God are open, and if not, see what you can do to re-open them by talking to Him. He's just waiting for you !

Further Study: Romans 8:28-30; Isaiah 42:8-9

Application: God is always ready to answer us when we call out to Him. He's not too keen on shopping lists, but He will always respond to a true cry from the heart. Why not give Him a call today?

פֶּסַח ב׳

Pesach - Passover - 2

Shemot/Exodus 15:1 I will sing to the Lord for He is highly exalted

אָשִׁירָה לַיהוה כִּי־גָאֹה גָּאָה

ga'ah ga'oh kiy l'Adonai ashiyrah

The last two words of the text show an interesting Hebrew construction. גָאֹה is a *Qal* infinitive, meaning 'to exalt', and גָּאָה is a *Qal* Affix 3ms form, meaning 'he exalted'. Together, the repeated verb indicates extreme intensity, a sense of maximum possible effect, giving a translation like "for He is supremely exalted". *Targum Onkelos* renders it as "He exalted Himself above those who are exalted, and exaltation is His", either referring to anyone or anything else, perhaps in the spiritual realm, that is exalted or has exalted itself, or to Pharaoh and the Egyptians who had exalted themselves above the peoples around them and against God.

An alternative, suggested by Rashi, is that the root meaning of the verb is 'to grow, to raise up' and the repetition indicates something that could not be done by another. No-one could properly exalt *HaShem*, He had to do it for Himself. The same verb is used in Isaiah 12:5 גֵּאוּת עָשָׂה, literally "he has made/done an exaltation", "He has done excellent things" (NASB). There are many places in Scripture where we find God doing things for Himself, because man won't or can't do them, such as "I sought for a man among them who could build a barricade or stand in the break to oppose Me on behalf of the land, so that I would not destroy it; but I found no-one" (Ezekiel 22:30, CJB). Isaiah continues, "I looked, but there was no-one to help Me, and I was appalled that no-one upheld Me. Therefore My own arm brought Me salvation" (Isaiah 63:5, CJB).

There are some things that only God can do. Only God could free our people from slavery and bring them out of Egypt. As we sing at the *Seder - Dayenu*, it would have been sufficient! But He brought us out, as He promised Moshe, "with an outstretched arm and great judgements" (Shemot 6:7). God demonstrated that the Egyptian gods were all non-entities and roundly discredited them. The Egyptians who pursued us were drowned in the Sea of Suf (the Sea of Reeds), in full view of our people, so that we would know that this was no accident, but the deliberate plan and purpose of God. Then He took us to Mt. Sinai, gave us the *Torah* and entered into covenant with us, that we would know how to be a holy people and serve Him.

But even that wasn't enough - the problem of sin remained. The Passover when we left Egypt was partly only a picture of what was yet to come: the defeat of sin and death, once and for all. This was so large that only God could do it; only He could plan and execute the means of rescuing mankind from the power of sin and death. Spoken of many times by the prophets, it was Yeshua - God Himself, not a messenger, an angel or a seraph - who came to be our *Pesach* sacrifice. "Therefore also God highly exalted Him, and bestowed upon Him the name which is above every name, that at the name of Yeshua, every knee should bow" (Philippians 2:9-10, NASB).

Further Study: Isaiah 45:20-25; Psalm 98:1-3; Hebrews 2:14-15

Application: As we work our way through the week of unleavened bread, eating the "humble bread" that our forefathers ate, let us remember that it is God who is exalted and as we eat, we act out again the prophecy that spoke of Yeshua and we look for the great redemption to come!

פֶּסַח ׳ג

Pesach - Passover - 3

Shemot/Exodus 12:3 They shall take - each man - a lamb for a fathers' house, a lamb for a household

וְיִקְחוּ לָהֶם אִישׁ שֶׂה לְבֵית־אָבֹת שֶׂה לַבָּיִת:

labayit   seh   avot   l'beyt   seh   iysh   lahem   v'yit'khu

There is some debate as to how many lambs were required for how many people because of this particular instruction. Rashi explains that בֵית־אָבֹת, fathers' house, is the same as 'family' from the parallel instruction in verse 21 below when Moshe actually gives this instruction to the people. The Mekhilta points out that both "fathers' house" and "family" refer to extended family units, whereas the second use of the word בָּיִת in this verse means an individual household. Rashi asks what would happen if the extended family were too large or numerous, so that there might not be sufficient for each to eat enough, then answers his own question by showing that this is why the "a lamb for a household" phrase is present - so that each distinct household - mother, father and children - even if part of a larger extended family grouping - should take their own lamb so that there was blood on the doorpost of every house and enough lamb for all to eat.

In the same way as *HaShem* instructs Moshe that each man is to take a lamb, the prophet Jeremiah again presents God's call for individual relationship: "In those days people will no longer say: 'The parents have eaten sour grapes, but their children's teeth are set on edge.' Rather, each person will die for his own sins. The teeth of every man who eats sour grapes will be set on edge" (Jeremiah 31:28-29, Living Nach). While still being within the nation of Israel and a part of God's covenant people, each individual person is responsible for their own actions and their own relationship with God. The text continues: "Rather, this is the covenant that I will make with the House of Israel after those days, says God: I will set My Torah among them and inscribe it on their hearts. I will be their God, and they will be My people. No longer will one person have to teach his fellow man and his brother, 'Know God!' for they will all know Me, says God, from the least of them to the greatest of them" (vv. 32-33, Living Nach). Clearly set within the context of a corporate relationship with Israel as a people, each person is to know God individually.

Yeshua, who is our *Pesach* - our Passover sacrifice (1 Corinthians 5:7) - emphasised that following Him is a personal action: "If anyone wishes to come after Me, let him deny himself, and take up his cross daily, and follow Me" (Luke 9:23, NASB). Whether wild or natural branches, we are grafted by faith into the olive tree of God's covenant relationship (Romans 11:11-24), but in both cases, the mechanism is by each person personally accepting God's offer of salvation: "If you confess with your mouth Yeshua as Lord, and believe in your heart that God raised Him from the dead, you shall be saved" (Romans 10:9, NASB) and that is the teaching of the whole of Scripture.

Further Study: Ezekiel 33:10-16; Romans 11:22-24

Application: Where do you stand today? Are you relying on the group of people - church or congregation - of which you are a part, or have you personally taken a lamb - The Lamb - and made peace with God? This Passover season, be sure that you know God's salvation for yourself, because God has no grand-children!

פֶּסַח ד׳

Pesach - Passover - 4

Shemot/Exodus 12:29 And it was at midnight and Adonai struck all the firstborn in the land of Egypt

וַיְהִי | בַּחֲצִי הַלַּיְלָה וַיהוה הִכָּה כָל־בְּכוֹר

b'chor chol hikah v'Adonai halaylah bakhatziy vay'hiy

בְּאֶרֶץ מִצְרָיִם

Mitzrayim b'eretz

The *Pesikta de Rab Kahana* connects this passage to King David: "At midnight I will rise to give thanks to You because of your judgements of mercy" (Psalm 119:62). "R. Phinehas said in the name of R. Eleazar bar R. Menahem: What did David do? He used to take a psaltery and a harp, put them at the head of his couch, and rising at midnight would play upon them. Thereupon the studious in Israel, upon hearing David's playing, used to say: 'If David, the king, occupies himself at midnight with *Torah*, so much the more should we.' And so it turned out that all in Israel occupied themselves with *Torah*." (Piska 7:4).

In another psalm, attributed to David when he was hiding in the cave from King Saul, David says, "Awake my glory; awake harp and lyre; I will awaken the dawn!" (Psalm 57:8, NASB). David declares that he will not wait for the dawn to awaken him, but by being awake and praising God he will awaken the dawn. To borrow Rav Sha'ul's words, he will "use the time well, for these are evil days" (Ephesians 5:16, CJB). Not knowing what the day might bring as Saul's men pursued him, always on the move, David made the most of every opportunity to praise God and spend time in His presence.

When the time came for Yeshua to be arrested, after His last *Pesach* meal with His disciples, Yeshua took the disciples out to the Garden of the Oil Press (Gethsemane). There He told them, "My anguish is so great that I feel as if I'm dying. Wait here and stay awake" (Mark 14:34, GWT). He went a little further and prayed but, "He went back and found them asleep. He said to Peter, 'Simon, are you sleeping? Couldn't you stay awake for one hour? Stay awake and pray that you won't be tempted'" (vv. 37-38, GWT). After a good meal and at least three cups of wine, it must have been difficult to stay awake. Yeshua went and prayed again but, "He found them asleep because they couldn't keep their eyes open. They didn't even know what they should say to Him" (v. 40, GWT). Yeshua wanted the disciples to stay awake and pray because midnight was approaching and they needed to be awake to witness His arrest and to be aware of what was going on, to be prepared for what was about to happen to Him.

Not everyone can be awake at midnight or before dawn every day, but there is a principle involved here. Rav Sha'ul, alluding to several passages from the prophet Isaiah, writes, "Get up sleeper! Arise from the dead, and the Messiah will shine on you!" (Ephesians 5:14, CJB). In the letter to the Thessalonians we find: "Let's not be asleep, like the rest are; on the contrary, let us stay alert and sober" (1 Thessalonians 5:6, CJB). Rav Sha'ul has been talking about the return of Messiah Yeshua, "the Day of the Lord" that will "come like a thief in the night" (v. 2, CJB) when people are not expecting Him. But we, just like our people about to leave Egypt over 3,500 years ago, have been given our orders. As we killed the lamb, daubed the blood on the doorposts and lintels of our houses, there must have been a growing excitement among our people; then we ate the roasted lamb in haste, with our robes tucked up ready for travel - "We're leaving Egypt tonight!" - and who could sleep, surely only the younger children. Then, before dawn, so early that we had to take our kneading troughs full of dough on our shoulders for want of time to bake it, we were off - following our God into the desert on the way to the Promised Land. "Since we belong to the day, let us stay sober, putting on trust and love as a breastplate and the hope of being delivered as a helmet" (1 Thessalonians 5:8, CJB).

Further Study: Isaiah 26:19, 52:1, 60:1; John 6:35-40

Application: Do you struggle with the - "yawn" - sameness of *Pesach* each year? If so, then shake yourself awake and use this time to connect with God at this important season. Set aside time during the week to praise God for the miracles He did for our forefathers; the miracles that He has done for us in Messiah Yeshua; and the miracle that He is yet to do for all those who believe and trust in Him at the Last Day.

פֶּסַח ה'

Pesach - Passover - 5

Shemot/Exodus 13:17 And it was when Pharaoh sent out the people

וַיְהִי בְּשַׁלַּח פַּרְעֹה אֶת־הָעָם
ha'am   et   Par'oh   b'shallakh vay'hiy

The word בְּשַׁלַּח is composed of בְּ, a preposition most often translated 'in', and the *Pi'el* infinitive construct of the verb root שָׁלַח, which in its *Qal* stem means 'to send'. Here the *Pi'el* stem has the meaning "to send out, send away", while the combination of the preposition with the infinitive form is considered to be a temporal reference, hence "when ... sent out". This is the opening verse of the portion *B'Shalach*, normally read 12 or so weeks ago, often in January on the Gregorian calendar.

In *Pesikta de Rab Kahana*, the rabbis connect this to the verse "When a man's ways please the Lord, He makes even his enemies to be at peace with him" (Proverbs 16:7). They considered "a man" to be Israel, referred to in the verse "every man of Israel" (1 Samuel 17:24) and "his enemy" to be Pharaoh, as the verse "The enemy said, 'I will pursue, I will overtake, I will divide the spoil'" (Shemot 15:9). They point out that although when Moshe first came to Pharaoh to say: "Thus says Adonai: Let My people go, then they may serve Me" (Shemot 8:16), Pharaoh - the wicked one - replied, "Who is Adonai, that I should hearken unto His voice? I know not Adonai, and moreover I will not let Israel go" (Shemot 5:2), but later exclaimed in repentance, "Adonai is righteous, and I and my people are wicked" (Shemot 9:27) and eventually sent Israel away, "Go in peace, go in peace!"

In reporting God's concern about the unjust behaviour of Israel, Micah sounds an alarming note: "Recently My people have arisen as an enemy" (Micah 2:8, NASB) because of the way they were treating strangers and widows. Even Israel, God's chosen people, can become God's enemies by disobeying Him; how much more those who do not know God. James goes as far as saying that, "whoever wishes to be a friend of the world makes himself an enemy of God" (James 4:4, NASB). Given the way the Scriptures speak of God's attitude to His enemies - "Let God arise, let His enemies be scattered; and let those who hate Him flee before Him. As smoke is driven away, to drive them away; as wax melts before the fire, so let the wicked perish before God" (Psalm 68:1-2, NASB) - this is a place that no-one wants to be, but how do we avoid being God's enemies? And once there, how can we get out of it again?

At this time of *Pesach*, we rehearse the lessons in the *Seder* and remember how God Himself rescued our people from Egypt. We see how *Pesach* is a vivid portrayal of the way that God would again intervene in human affairs to rescue us from a far worse situation than physical slavery in Egypt, spiritual bondage to sin, by sending Messiah Yeshua to be our *Pesach*, our Passover Lamb. "For while we were still helpless, at the right time, the Messiah died on behalf of ungodly people" (Romans 5:6, CJB). God knew exactly where we were and what we were capable of, so Rav Sha'ul continues, "we were reconciled with God through His Son's death when we were enemies" (v. 10, CJB). God wanted - still wants - to be reconciled with us, His enemies, so He broke through the barrier that we could not, in order to achieve reconciliation. "For it pleased God to have His full being live in His Son and through His Son to reconcile to Himself all things, whether on earth or in heaven, making peace through Him, through having His Son shed His blood by being executed on a stake" (Colossians 1:19-20, CJB).

Just as the message of the *Haggadah* is "Come and eat; let all who are hungry come and eat" - drawing on Isaiah 55 - so God's message is for all people, "because we are convinced that one man died on behalf of all mankind" (2 Corinthians 5:14, CJB) and has commissioned us to share that message with others: "And it is all from God, who through the Messiah has reconciled us to Himself and has given us the work of that reconciliation" (v. 18 CJB). We have this charge on our lives, to spread the word of reconciliation to all people and to be reconciled with each other. Remember the words of Yeshua: "If you are offering your gift at the Temple altar and you remember there that your brother has something against you, leave your gift where it is by the altar, and go, make peace with your brother. Then come back and offer your gift" (Matthew 5:23-24, CJB). Our reconciliation with God is incomplete unless we have reconciled with our brother and settled whatever they have against us.

Further Study: Isaiah 53:4-6; 1 John 2:15-17

Application: Are you at peace with your neighbour, reconciled to your brother, whether your physical or spiritual family? This Passover season, take the time to fully experience God's reconciliation by making sure that you have extended it to others.

פֶּסַח ו׳

Pesach - Passover - 6

Shemot/Exodus 11:5 And all the first-born in the land of Egypt shall die ... and all the first-born of cattle.

וּמֵת כָּל־בְּכוֹר בְּאֶרֶץ מִצְרַיִם ... וְכֹל בְּכוֹר

b'chor v'chol ... Mitzrayim b'eretz b'chor kol oomeyt

בְּהֵמָה:

b'heymah

We know that God is merciful, for the Scriptures tell us that "it is not His purpose that anyone should be destroyed, but that everyone should turn from his sins" (2 Peter 3:9, CJB), so how are we to make sense of our text? Does that not appear to be a fairly all-encompassing sentence upon a huge number of people? Indeed, the early rabbis taught that the first-born were not only the first-born of man but also of woman and that the first-born child could be of either male or female gender, thus including an even broader range - almost everyone seems to be included one way or another. Perhaps that is why the narrative of the first Passover night's fulfillment of the text says: "and there was a great cry in Egypt, for there was no house where there was not someone dead" (Shemot 12:30, NASB). In Pesikta de Rab Kahana the rabbis pick up on the last phrase of our text and ask, "Men sinned, to be sure, but how can cattle be said to have sinned?" They then provide the answer, "Since the Egyptians worshiped the ram - the symbol of the Egyptian god Amon, whom the Greeks identified with Zeus - the cattle were also struck in order that the Egyptians should not be able to say: It is our deity who has brought thus punishment upon us. Our deity is strong and can stand up for himself, as is shown by the fact that this punishment did not come upon such animals as represent him" (Piska 7).

The rabbis use the progression of *tzara'at* as another example of the way in which *HaShem* is reluctant to harm mankind. First, He begins with a man's house; if he repents then only those stones affected by the *tzara'at* need be removed: "then the priest shall order them to tear out the stones with the mark in them and throw them away at an unclean place outside the city" (Vayikra 14:40, NASB). But if he does not repent, then the whole house has to be broken down: "He shall therefore tear down the house, its stones and its timbers, and all the plaster of the house, and he shall take them outside the city to an unclean place" (v. 45, NASB). Next, the focus shifts to the man's clothes; if a man repents, then only a patch is torn from the garment: "then if the priest shall look and if the mark has faded after it has been washed, then he shall tear it out of the garment" (13:56, NASB). But if he does not repent then the whole garment is lost: "the article with the mark shall be burned in the fire" (v. 57, NASB). Finally, if He has not had a response, *HaShem* turns to the man's body; if he repents then he is cured of the *tzara'at* in his flesh. If he still refuses to repent then "he shall remain unclean all the days during which he has the infection; he is unclean. He shall live alive; his dwelling shall be outside the camp" (13:46, NASB).

The same progression is also seen in the way that *HaShem* allows Job to be tested by Satan - first only his possessions and family: "Behold, all that he has is in your power, only do not put forth your hand on him" (Job 1:12, NASB). Only when Job proves that he will not sin or blame God is Satan empowered to move further: "Behold, he is in your power, only spare his life" (2:6, NASB); his life is protected throughout. The rabbis see a similar progression in the treatment of Elimelech and his sons at the start of the story of Ruth (Ruth 1:3,5) and quote from the Psalms to show the process at work in the Egyptian plagues - crops, cattle, mankind: "He struck down their vines also and the fig trees, and shattered the trees of their territory" (Psalm 105:33, NASB), "He gave over their cattle also to the hailstones, and their herds to bolts of lightening" (Psalm 78:48, NASB); only at the last did *HaShem* resort to touching man: "And [He] smote all the first-born in Egypt" (v. 51, NASB).

God acts in the same way with believers and those who do not know Him today. There are many powerful testimony books that show how God patiently pursued a man or a woman through years of sinful living and rebellion before finally catching up with them: "He wants all humanity to be delivered and come to full knowledge of the truth" (1 Timothy 2:4, CJB). God has a vision and a plan for each of our lives, so the prophet said, "For the vision is meant for its appointed time; it speaks of the end, and it does not lie. It may take a while, but wait for it; it will surely come, it will not delay" (Habakkuk 2:3, CJB). Although men may put God "on the back-burner", "you despise the riches of his kindness, forbearance and patience; because you don't realize that God's kindness is intended to lead you to turn from your sins" (Romans 2:4, CJB), it is absolutely certain that He will be there waiting for them, either in this world or the next! He closes down our options so that we have to focus on Him.

This position applies also to believers. As Peter writes, "For the time has come for the judgment to begin. It begins with the household of God" (1 Peter 4:17, CJB). God wants us too to repent of our sinful ways and habits so that we may be cleansed and purified by His grace and forgiveness. Speaking of disputes within the body, Yeshua taught a staged approach: "Moreover, if your brother commits a sin against you, go and show him his fault - but privately, just between the two of you. If he listens to you, you have won back your brother. If he doesn't listen, take one or two others with you so that every accusation can be supported by the testimony of two or three witnesses. If he refuses to hear them, tell the congregation; and if he refuses to listen even to the congregation, treat him as you would a pagan or a tax-collector" (Matthew 18:15-17, CJB). He also taught that our forgiveness from God is conditioned upon our forgiveness from those we have offended.

Writing to the Corinthian community, Rav Sha'ul told them, "Get rid of the old hametz, so that you can be a new batch of dough, because in reality you are unleavened. For our Pesach lamb, the Messiah, has been sacrificed. So let us celebrate the Seder not with leftover hametz, the hametz of wickedness and evil, but with the matzah of purity and truth" (1 Corinthians 5:7-8, CJB). Sha'ul is pointing to two things here. Firstly, as believers in Messiah, we are in relationship with God, we are new creations, Yeshua has already justified us with God so that we are free to serve Him. We are no longer slaves to sin; we have a choice in our behaviour and speech. Secondly, Sha'ul urges us to celebrate, not just the Passover *seder* at this particular time of year, but throughout the year, our freedom in Messiah. We can do and say good things; we can choose always to speak the truth; we can live lives that are pure from the contamination of the world. Both as individuals and as a community we can celebrate this Passover season in a righteous way that will be more pleasing to God than last year.

Further Study: Shemot 13:6-7; Ephesians 4:22-24

Application: How can you move towards purity and truth in your life this Passover season? Perhaps you could prune your library of videos with any rating higher than PG, or put out any books that you wouldn't want your children or grandchildren to read. Activities that you wouldn't want to take Yeshua along to are an obvious candidate for stopping, as are relationships or habits that drag you down or away from God. As we focus on removing leaven from our houses, why not remove some from your life!

פֶּסַח ז׳

Pesach - Passover - 7

Yesha'yahu/Isaiah 60:2 For behold, darkness will cover [the] earth and a thick cloud the peoples; but on you Adonai will rise and His glory will be seen upon you.

כִּי־הִנֵּה הַחֹשֶׁךְ יְכַסֶּה־אֶרֶץ וַעֲרָפֶל לְאֻמִּים
l'oomiym   v'arafel   eretz y'chaseh hakhoshech hiney kiy

וְעָלַיִךְ יִזְרַח יהוה וּכְבוֹדוֹ עָלַיִךְ יֵרָאֶה:
yeyra'eh alayich   uch'vodo Adonai yizrakh v'alayich

The verb יְכַסֶּה, a *Pi'el* prefix 3ms form from the root כָּסָה - to cover or conceal - is the only verb in the first half of the verse, doing duty for both the darkness covering the earth and the thick cloud or gloom that covers the peoples or nations. By contrast, two different verbs are present in the second half: יִזְרַח, a *Qal* prefix 3ms form of זָרַךְ - to rise, as the sun - and יֵרָאֶה, a *Niphal* prefix 3ms form of רָאָה - to see. The use of prefix verbs - denoting incomplete action - throughout the verse marks this as future or predictive text and the wider context of the chapter makes this clear: Isaiah is speaking words of comfort for the people of Judah just before the Babylonian exile, to assure them that Jerusalem does have a future and that God will return to show favour to His people.

In *Pesikta de Rab Kahana*, the ancient rabbis connected this verse to the ninth of the ten plagues with which *HaShem* afflicted the Egyptians in order to set Israel free.

"R. Aha bar Kahana said: For three days darkness and thick darkness [תֹהוּ וָבֹהוּ, cf. B'resheet 1:2] were called upon to serve in Egypt. The proof is the verse, 'And there was a thick darkness in all the land of Egypt for three days' (Shemot 10:22). On the other hand, dark chaos and emptiness have never been summoned to serve in this world, but where will they be called into service? In the great city of Rome: 'He shall stretch over it the line of [dark] chaos, and the plumbline of emptiness' (Isaiah 34:11)."

The Isaiah verse was originally given in an oracle against Edom, which has long been used by the rabbis as a synonym for Rome: first in ancient times meaning the Roman empire which had destroyed the Temple, ploughed Jerusalem with salt and martyred the sages in order to suppress Judaism, but since then to refer to the organised church which was responsible for pogroms and persecution of the Jewish people, the crusades and the Inquisition. Edom/Rome was considered insufferably proud and arrogant, crushing others and brushing aside the truth in its pursuit of a birthright which was no longer theirs.

The rabbinic chorus then takes over from Rabbi Aha:

"The nations of the earth which have not accepted the *Torah* that was given out of darkness [over Sinai], of them Scripture says, 'Behold, darkness shall cover the earth, and gross darkness the peoples' (Isaiah 60:2). But Israel, who accepted the *Torah* that was given out of darkness, of them Scripture says, 'But upon you the Lord will rise, and His glory shall be seen upon you' (ibid.)."

The nations, those who do not recognise or obey the *Torah*, will be in that darkness, will experience that chaos; Israel, God's chosen people, and those who join her in obeying the *Torah*, will bask in God's presence and His glory will be evident among them. Egypt was cast down because they refused to acknowledge *HaShem* - יהוה - and so they went though an intense period of darkness and chaos, to shake them and destroy their self-confidence. Israel, who followed the instructions for the *Pesach* offering - the blood of the lamb on the lintel and doorposts of their houses - not only had light when the Egyptians were in a darkness so thick it could be felt, but were set free from their slavery to follow the pillar of cloud and fire - a physical manifestation of God - as He led them through the desert towards the Promised Land.

Pesach is one of those times in the year, perhaps a unique time, to decide where we stand. The *Torah* is clear about the celebration of *Pesach*: "All the congregation of Israel are to celebrate this ... but no uncircumcised person may eat of it" (Shemot 12:47-48, NASB). Those who are not circumcised, whether Israelite or a stranger - however righteous or not - are not considered part of Israel and are not allowed to eat the meal. The Christian world celebrates communion as the reality of which *Pesach* is the shadow; a weekly remembering of the death and resurrection of Yeshua in the *matzah* and cup that followed the meal in Yeshua's last *Pesach Seder* with His *talmidim* - the cup of redemption. Using the *kol va'chomer* argument, if only those who are circumcised physically are allowed to eat the *Pesach* meal, how much more so those who come to the Lord's table to share the symbols of His body and blood. Rav Sha'ul clearly has that in view when he warns the Corinthians not to eat or drink unworthily lest "he who eats and drinks, eats and drinks judgment to himself" (1 Corinthians 11:29, NASB).

Since circumcision, at least for religious purposes, is forbidden to Gentiles (cf. Acts 15:19-20, Galatians 5:2-4), how are Gentile believers in Yeshua ever to participate in communion or attend a *Seder*? Rav Sha'ul again: "For he is not a Jew who is one outwardly; neither is circumcision that which is outward in the flesh. But he is a Jew who is one inwardly; and circumcision is that which is of the heart, by the Spirit, not by the letter; and his praise is not from men, but from God" (Romans 2:28-29, NASB). Understand Sha'ul clearly here: he is not talking about whether Jewish men or boys should be circumcised, that is a given as a simple matter of who they are; neither is he proposing some kind of "spiritual Jew" who is somehow Jewish without being circumcised; nor is is he suggesting that all Gentile believers are really Jewish because they have come to faith in Yeshua. No, he is talking about those who will be counted as righteous in keeping God's covenant and so are entitled to eat from God's table. As David says: "Who may ascend unto the hill of the Lord? And who may stand in His holy place? He who has clean hands and a pure heart" (Psalm 24:3-4, NASB); clean hands and a pure heart come only through Yeshua.

On the day of *Pesach* we also start the week of *matzah*, unleavened bread. For seven days we eat the poor bread, cooked so quickly that it does not have time to rise. The rabbis teach that bread containing *chametz* - leaven, yeast - symbolises pride and arrogance for it is all puffed up and full of itself. Rav Sha'ul echoes that when he writes of "the chametz of wickedness and evil" (1 Corinthians 5:8, CJB). The simple unleavened bread, is therefore known as the bread of humility, "the matzah of purity and truth" (ibid.). A week of eating *matzah*, with its hard edges and sharp corners, is quite a lesson to the mouth which can be applied in a very real spiritual sense. For the Jew who does not yet believe in Yeshua, this lesson is particularly poignant: will we humble ourselves, in spite of our millennia of tradition and the *Torah* that we keep and teach, in order to eat the bread of humility and accept the One who said: "I am the bread of life; he who comes to Me shall not hunger, and he who believes in Me shall never thirst" (John 6:35, NASB)? Rabbi Aha's text seems clear: do we want God to lay out over us His plumbline of darkness and chaos, because we refused to accept the Living *Torah*, or do we want God Himself to rise over us and display His glory once again in our midst?

Chag *Pesach* Sameach!

Further Study: Isaiah 55:1-3; Ezekiel 10:4; Ephesians 4:17-20

Application: *Pesach* comes once a year, preceded by four weeks of fervent and serious house cleaning. We expose all the dark corners of our homes in order to remove all the *chametz* to the light. The days before *Pesach* provide an opportunity to expose the inner recesses of our lives - particularly the little fusty corners where pride can ferment and grow - to the light of Messiah. Let's have a real clean out this year so that we can celebrate the *Seder* in truth!

Biographies

Abravanel - Don Isaac Abravanel, 1437-1508, Statesman and biblical commentator; born in Lisbon, died in Venice; claimed descent from King David; wrote commentaries on the whole of the Hebrew Scriptures

Ba'al HaTurim - Rabbi Yaakov ben Asher, 1269-1343, born in Cologne, Germany; lived for 40 years in and around Toledo, Spain; died *en route* to Israel; his commentary to the Chumash is based upon an abridgement of the Ramban, including Rashi and Ibn Ezra; it includes many references to *gematria* and textual novelties

Bechor Schor - Joseph ben Isaac Bekhor Shor of Orleans, a French tosafist, exegete, and poet who flourished in the 2nd half of the 12th century.

Buber - Martin Buber, 1878-1965, born in Austria, a Jewish philosopher; emigrated to Israel in 1938 and taught at the Hebrew University

Chizkuni - Rabbi Hezekiah ben Manoah (13th century), French rabbi and exegete; his commentary on the *Torah* was written about 1240 in memory of his father, based principally on Rashi, but using about 20 other sources

Chofetz Chaim - Rabbi Israel Meir Kagan, 1838-1933, rabbi and Rosh Yeshiva in Radin (was Poland, now Belarus); famous for his first book about gossip and slander

Gersonides - Rabbi Levi ben Gershom, Gersonides or Ralbag, 1288-1344; famous rabbi, philosopher, mathematician and astronomer/astrologer; born at Bagnols in Languedock, France; wrote a commentary on the *Torah* and a parallel to Maimonides' Guide For The Perplexed

Hirsch - Rabbi Samson Raphael Hirsch, 1808-1888, German rabbi of Frankfurt am Main, author and educator; staunch opponent of the Reform movement in Germany and one of the fathers of Orthodox Judaism

Ibn Ezra - Abraham Ibn Ezra, 1089-1167, born in Tudela, Spain; died in the South of France after wandering all around the shores of the Mediterranean and England; a philosopher, astronomer, doctor, poet and linguist; wrote a Hebrew grammar and a commentary on the Bible

Nechama Leibowitz - 1905-1997, born in Riga, graduate of the University of Berlin, made *aliyah* in 1931; professor at Tel Aviv University; taught *Torah* for over 50 years

S D Luzzatto - Samuel David Luzzatto, 1880-1865, was an Italian Jewish scholar and poet; one of the first Jewish scholars to suggest critical emendations to the biblical text

Rabbi Akiva - Akiva ben Joseph, c.50-c.135; one of the third generation of the Mishnaic Sages, who were active between 70 and 135; although starting life as an ignorant shepherd, he became perhaps the most central authority quoted in the Mishnah; known by some as the "father of the Rabbinic Judaism"

Ramban - Rabbi Moshe ben Nachman of Gerona or Nachmanides, 1194-1270, Spanish rabbi, author and physician; defended Judaism in the Christian debates in Barcelona before making *aliyah* to *Eretz Yisrael*

Ramchal - Moshe Chaim Luzzatto, 1707-1746; a prominent Italian rabbi, kabbalist, and philosopher

Rashbam - Rabbi Shmuel ben Meir, 1085-1158, born in Troyes, France; grandson of Rashi; his commentaries focus on the *p'shat* (plain) meaning of the text

Rashi - Rabbi Shlomo Yitzchaki, 1040-1105, French rabbi who wrote commentaries on the *Torah*, the Prophets and the Talmud, lived in Troyes where he founded a *yeshiva* in 1067; perhaps the best-known of all Jewish commentators; focuses on the plain meaning (*p'shat*) of the text, although sometimes quite cryptic in his brevity

Sforno - Rabbi Ovadiah Sforno, 1470-1550, Italian rabbi, philosopher and physician; born in Cesena, he went to Rome to study medicine; left in 1525 and after some years of travel, settled in Bologna where he founded a *yeshiva* which he conducted until his death

Bibliography

Books by Author

Benjamin Davidson, *The Analytical Hebrew and Chaldee Lexicon*, Samuel Bagster & Sons Ltd, London 1850

Brown, Driver and Briggs, *Hebrew and English Lexicon*, HoughtonMiflin and Company, Boston 1906

William L. Holladay, *A Concise Hebrew and Aramaic Lexicon of the Old Testament*, Eerdmans, Grand Rapids, MI, 1971

Israel Drazin & Stanley M Wagner, *Onkelos on the Torah - Leviticus*, Gefen Publishing House, Jerusalem 2008

Martin Goodman, *Rome and Jerusalem*, Penguin/Allen Lane, 2007

Richard Elliott Friedman, *Commentary on the Torah*, Harper Collins, San Francisco 2003

Simon J. Kistemaker, *The Parables - Understanding the Stories Jesus Told*, Baker, Grand Rapids, MI, 2002

Baruch Levine, *The JPS Torah Commentary - Leviticus*, Jewish Publication Society, Philadephia 1989

John Ortberg, *Love Beyond Reason*, Zondervan, Grand Rapids, MI, 1998

Derek Prince, *Bought with Blood: the Divine Exchange at the Cross*, Chosen Books, 0800794249

Derek Prince, *The Divine Exchange*, Derek Prince Ministries UK, 1997

Nahum Sarna, *The JPS Torah Commentary - Exodus*, Jewish Publication Society, Philadephia 1989

David Wenham, *The Parables of Jesus*, IVP, Downers Grove, Illinois, 1989

Brad H. Young, *The Parables - Jewish Tradition and Christian Interpretation*, Hendrickson, Peabody, Massachusetts, 1998

Books by Title

Akedat Yitzckah - a length philosophical commentary on the *Torah* by Isaac ben Moses Arama (c.1420 - 1494), a Spanish rabbi and author

Artscroll Siddur - one of the "standard" siddur texts available today, published by Mesorah Publications Ltd, Brooklyn, New York, 1984-99

Avot de Rabbi Natan - described as a commentary to *Pirkei Avot* (a tractate of the Mishnah); written between 700 and 900 CE; in style a mixture of *Mishnah* and *Midrash*

BHS - Biblia Hebraica Stuttgartensia, the standard eclectic/scholarly text of the Hebrew Scriptures, German Bible Society 1997

Guide for the Perplexed - one of the major works by Maimonides, the Rambam; written in the 12th century in the form of a three-volume letter to his student, Rabbi Joseph ben Judah of Ceuta; a major work of Jewish philosophy

Hertz Siddur - a older "standard" siddur text: Joseph H. Hertz, *The Authorised Daily Prayer Book*, Blochm New York, 1975

Living Nach - part of a series of books starting with the *Living Torah* (1 volume) and the *Living Nach* (3 volumes); a contemporary yet traditional translation of the Hebrew Scriptures into English started by Rabbi Aryeh Kaplan and finished in his style by others rabbinicscholars; published by Moznaim Publishing Corporation, Brooklyn, NY, 1981-98

Mekhilta - The earliest known halachic *midrash* or commentary on (parts of) the book of Exodus; formally named for Rabbi Ishmael and therefore set around 100-135CE, it was redacted some years after his time; quoted many times in the Bavli Talmud as "Rabbi Ishmael taught ..."

Midrash Rabbah - a collection of *aggadic* commentaries upon the *Torah* and some other books of the Bible most used in worship; different volumes have been collated in written form between the 4th and 13th centuries CE; they contain both very early oral material from the sages of the 1st and 2nd centuries and glosses and inserts down to the 1200s

Mishnah - the collection of Jewish Law and custom codified (collected and written down) under the auspices of Rabbi Judah the Prince around the year 200 CE

Mizrachi - a super-commentary on Rashi written by Elijah Mizrachi, 1455-1525, born in Constantinople, in 1495 became Grand Rabbi of the Ottoman empire

Passover Hagaddah - literally, "The Tellling"; the order of words used to conduct the Passover *Seder* each year; contains tradition material that may date from Second Temple times; codified around 200 CE, some suggest by Rabbi Judah himself

Pesikta de Rab Kahana - a collection of *midrash* and sermons for the special sabbaths and the festivals throughout the year; the oldest material comes from the 1st and 2nd centuries but the collection was probably redacted in the late 4th or early 5th century

Sefer Zikaron - a super-commentary on Rashi, by Avraham Bokrat, Jerusalem 1967

Sefer HaChinuch - Simply, "The Book of Education"; a systematic discussion of the 613 commandments; published anonymously in 13th century Spain; sometimes ascribed to Rabbi Aharon HaLevi of Barcelona (1235 - c.1290)

Septuagint - Also known simply as LXX, the Septuagint is a translation of the whole of the Hebrew Scriptures into Greek that was probably done during the 1st century BCE by members of the Jewish community in Alexandria to have the Scriptures in their "first" tongue; the quality is mixed - some parts, such as the *Torah*, were in frequent use and are quite well rendered, other parts were less used and the translation is rather patchy and shows signs of haste; it was widely deprecated by the early rabbis who generated the story of its being translated under threat of death by 70 Jewish scholars on the orders of Ptolemy

Sifra - the earliest rabbinic commentary to the book of Vayikra; probably redacted by Rabbi Khiyya with additions by the the School of Rabbi Ishmael; quoted extensively in the Talmud, the whole shows a distinct Judean rather than Babylonian tradition; the earliest material dates from 100-150 CE, but there are later additions

Sifre - the earliest rabbinic commentary to the books of B'Midbar and D'varim; probably composed of two parts, one from the Schools of Rabbi Simeon and Rabbi Ishmael, the other from the School of Rabbi Akiva; the earliest material dates from 100-150 CE, but there are later additions until *Talmudic* times

Sifsei Chachamim - a super-commentary to Rashi's commentary on the Pentateuch; written by Shabbetai ben Joseph Bass, 1641-1718, an educated man and printer of Jewish books in Breslau

Talmud - literally, instruction or learning; the distilled writings of the early sages, a composite of the Mishnah and the *Gemarah* - an extensive commentary to the Mishnah; two talmuds exist: the Jerusalem Talmud, from around 400-450 CE, compiled in the Land of Israel; and the Babylonian Talmud, from around 550-600 CE, compiled in the Jewish communities in Babylon

Tanakh - the Hebrew Scriptures: *Torah* (Instructions/Law), *Nevi'im* (Prophets) and *Ketuvim* (Writings)

Torat Kohanim - an alternative name for Sifra

Vayikra Rabbah - one of the components of the Midrash Rabbah collection (the Great Midrash), probably compiled between the 5th and 7th centuries CE in *Eretz Yisrael* from the oral teachings of many of the early sages - some named, some anonymous - in the previous 400 - 700 years

Vulgate - a translation of both the Hebrew and greek Scriptures to Latin that was undertaken - at least in significant part - by Jerome between 382-405 CE; it was unusual in being a fresh translation from the best available Hebrew and Greek texts rather than working from the Septuagint; it does include some exegetical material and a rather paraphrased style

Glossary

Adonai - literally, "My Lord" or "My Master"; although appearing in the Hebrew text as a word in its own right, it is widely used as a elusive synonym to avoid pronouncing the tetragrammaton - יהוה - the ineffable or covenant name of God; where the latter appears in a text, and is being read in a worship context, it will be pronounced as *Adonai*

Akkadian - a semitic language, spoken in ancient Mesopotamia, particularly by the Babylonians and Assyrians, named from the city of Akkad, a major city of Mesopotamian civilisation. Written in cuneiform; spoken for several millenia but probably exinct by 100CE

aliyah (pl. *aliyot*) - literally "going up"; used as the name for one (or more) of the seven sections in which the *Torah* portion is read on *Shabbat*; so named because (1) the reader ascends physically to the *bimah* or platform in the synagogue to read and (2) the reader ascends spiritually by reading from the *Torah*

Amidah - The Standing Prayer, see *Shemoneh Esrei*

anthropomorphism - ascribing human qualities - emotions, attributes or physical characteristics - to God or an inanimate object

Avraham Avinu - literally, Abraham our father

B'rit Hadashah - literally, New Covenant

Chazal - an acronym: "Ch" stands for "Chachameinu", Our Sages, and the "z" and "l" correspond to the expression "Zichronam Livrocho", "of blessed memory"; this is a catch-all that often refers to the authoritative opinion in the Talmud, sometimes just the collected wisdom of the Sages in years past

chutzpah - the original Hebrew word means "insolence, audacity or impertinence"; colloquially, "nerve" or "gall"

cohen (pl. *cohanim*) - priest, so *cohen gadol* or *Cohen HaGadol*, the High Priest

Days of Awe - the ten (inclusive) days between *Yom Teruah* and *Yom*

Kippur

Diaspora - from a Greek word meaning to scatter or disperse, this is the name given to the Jewish people scattered in exile throughout the world, as opposed to the part of the Jewish people that live in *Eretz Yisrael*

Eretz Yisrael - the Land of Israel

gematria - a system of assigning a numerical value to a Hebrew word or phrase (using the numerical values of the letter) in order to connect it to other words and phrases having the same numerical value; produces some interesting results but can be abused to generate spurious connections

Haftarah - literally, "leave taking"; the reading from the Prophets or Writings that follows the reading from the *Torah*; thematically linked to the *Torah* reading, some of these have been set since the Babylonian exile

halacha - literally "the walking"; the detailed case law of implementing *Torah*

HaShem - literally, "The Name"; widely used as a elusive synonym to avoid pronouncing the tetragrammaton - יהוה - the ineffable or covenant name of God; where this appears in a text, and is not being read in a worship context, if will be pronounced as *HaShem*

Hif'il and *Hof'al* - the causitive voices (active and passive, respectively) of a Hebrew verb

Hitpa'el and *Hotpa'el* - the relexive or iterative voices (active and passive, respectively) of a Hebrew verb

Kaddish - most frequently Mourner's Kaddish, the prayer said by mourners during the prayer service during the first year after the death of a close family member; also the Rabbi's Kaddish, said at the end of or at intervals between study

kashrut - the Mosaic dietary laws

kol va'chomer - an argument style that moves from the lesser to the greater: if this small condition applies, how much more so when this greater condition applies *kosher* - literally, "approved"; something, typically food, that meets the appropriate regulations; the term *glatt kosher* (the Yiddish word *glatt* means 'smooth') is informally used to denote food prepared to the strictest *kosher* regulations

lashon hara - literally, "the evil tongue"; gossip or bad speech about someone or something

masorete - the Masoretes were groups of scribes and scholars in Tiberias and Jerusalem - *masorete* meaning guardian or keeper of tradition - in the 8th - 9th centuries CE; they preserved the traditional pronunciation, chanting and breathing of the Hebrew Bible text, lest it should be lost and future generations unable to read and interpret the consonantal text

Masoretic Text - the standard Jewish text of the Hebrew Bible, as annotated with vowels and trope marks by the *Masoretes* in the 9th century CE; devised by Aaron ben Moses ben Asher in Tiberias, these pointed texts are preserved in the Aleppo Codex (~930 CE) and the Leningrad Codex (1008 CE)

matzah (pl. *matzot*) - unleavened bread; flat bread made without yeast

Midrash (pl. *midrashim*) - literally, study or investigation; the technique of *Midrash* is to interpret or study texts based on textual issues, links to other verses and narratives; as a class it includes both *halachic* (law-based) and *aggadic* (story or narrative) material which often fills in many gaps in the biblical material

mikvah - pool with naturally running water for ritual washing

Mishkan - literally, "place of dwelling/presence"; the Tabernacle

Niphal - the passive voice of a Hebrew verb

parasha (pl. *parashiyot*) - one of the traditional names for the divisions into weekly portions of the Hebrew Bible; the *Torah* contains 54 portions, each with its own name taken from one of the first few words in the text

Parochet - the thick curtain that hung in the Temple as a division between the Holy Place - which was accessible to all priests throughout the year - and the Holy of Holies, where only the High Priest could go, once a year; described as being a cubit or more in thickness and decorated in rich colours and designs

Pesach - Passover

Pi'el and *Pu'al* - the emphatic or stressed voices (active and passive, respectively) of a Hebrew verb

P'rushim - Pharisees

Omer - literally, "sheaf"; a dry volume measure for grain; used for counting the fifty days of the barley harvest between *Pesach* and *Shavuot*

Qal - literally, "light"; the unmodified or unenhanced version of a Hebrew verb; the simplest meaning of a Hebrew verb root

Rosh Chodesh - literally, "head of the month"; the day of the New Moon feast, to be marked by the blowing of silver trumpets; declared by the *Sanhedrin* in Jerusalem after having received reliable testimony from two witnesses that the new moon has been sighted

Rosh HaShana - literally, "head of the year"; the first day of *Tishrei*, the seventh month in the Jewish year, also known as *Yom Teruah*, the Day of Blowing; used as the civil New Year

Ruach HaKodesh - literally, "Spirit or Breath, the Holy"; most common Hebrew name for the Holy Spirit; also *Ruach Elohim*, The Spirit of God

Sanhedrin - the most senior court in biblical Israel, with seventy one members; recently re-founded in the modern state of Israel

seder - literally, "order"; a formal liturgical remembrance and meal; most familiarly the Passover Seder, 3 hours of liturgy and ritual actions to remember the Exodus from Egypt; also *Shavuot* Seder and Tu B'Shevat Seder

sha'atnez - material or clothing that contains the prohibited mixture of both wool and linen

Shabbat - the 24 hours from sunset Friday to sunset Saturday, the seventh day of the week; literally, "the ceasing" because as Jews we cease any kind of work during those hours

Shabbat Sheckalim - the day each year when the half-shekel tax for the upkeep of the Temple was collected; now set as the *shabbat* before the first of Adar (Adar II in a leap year); the *Torah* portion Shemot 30:11-16

is read

Shabbat Shuva - the *shabbat* that falls between *Yom Teruah (Rosh HaShana)* and *Yom Kippur* each year; so called from the *Haftarah* portion which is read: Hosea 14:2-10, starting with the imperative verb *Shuva*, Return!

Shacharit - literally, "dawn"; the name of the early morning prayer service

Shavuot - literally "weeks"; the name of the biblical Feast of Weeks at the end of the fifty days of counting the *Omer* (sheaf) from *Pesach* (Passover)

Shemoneh Esrei - literally, "The Eighteen" because it originally contained eighteen stanzas or blessings; the central prayer of the three daily prayer services. Also known as the *Amidah* - "standing" or simply "the prayer", the rabbis determined that this prayer was the act of service that replaced the sacrifices in worship after the destruction of the Second Temple

shofar - a trumpet made from a ram's horn

sidra - another name for the portions of the *Torah*, from a root verb meaning "to order"; see *parasha*

talmid (pl. *talmidim*) - student or disciple

Tanna - Hebrew, literally, "repeater or teacher"; one of the rabbinic sages whose views are recorded in the Mishnah; active from around 70 - 200 CE

Targum - literally, translation or interpretation; two principle *targums* are known: *Targum Onkelos*, a translation with some paraphrase of the *Torah* into Aramaic; *Targum Jonathan*, a translation with rather more paraphrase of the Prophets into Aramaic. They were probably made between 200-400 and were used in the reading and study of the Hebrew scriptures: one line or verse in Hebrew, followed by the same line or verse from the *Targum*. Important early witnesses to the text and translation into a closely connected cognate language

tetragrammaton - the four letter covenant name of God: יהוה yod-hay-vav-hay; never pronounced as written within the Jewish tradition and never vowelised with a correct set of vowels to prevent pronunciation

Torah - the first in the three parts of the Hebrew Bible (with Prophets and Writings); from the root יָרָה, to throw or teach; often translated 'law' but probably better 'instruction'; used at a minimum to describe the five books of Moshe, often expanded to include the whole of the Hebrew Bible, the Talmud and the Jewish writings, so that it can be used as a totally encompassing term

tzara'at - Hebrew word for skin disease; often translated - incorrectly, since it bears no relationship to the latter disease - as leprosy

tziytziyt - tassles; worn (as per B'Midbar 15:38-40) on the four corners of a garment

Ugaritic - a semitic language, spoken in the city of Ugarit in Syria in the 14th - 12th centuries BCE, and written in cuneiform; lost when the city was destroyed in 1180/70 BCE; used by the Caananite culture, it has been important for Hebrew scholars in clarifying the meaning and use of common words, idioms and expressions

Urim & Thumim - a now unknown mechanism provided in the *Torah* for the priests to answer specific questions

yarhzeit (also spelled *yahrzeit*) - the anniversary of a person's death

Yom Kippur - the Day of Atonement

Author Biography

Although professionally trained and qualified as a software engineer, Jonathan's calling to the Messianic Jewish ministry started in the mid-90s after a season of serving as a local preacher in the churches of North Devon. He was ordained "Messianic Rabbi" by Dr Daniel Juster and Tikkun Ministries, and has served as a Tikkun network congregational leader in England for some years. Now the founder and director of Messianic Education Trust - an educational charity and ministry that works to share the riches of the Jewish background of our faith in Messiah with the church, while teaching Yeshua as the Jewish messiah - he lives in the south-west of England with his wife, Belinda, and three of his four daughters. There he contributes to the local body of believers by being involved in the Exeter Street Pastors project.

You can follow the work of Messianic Education Trust and read the weekly commentaries as they are produced each week, on the MET website at:

http://www.messianictrust.org

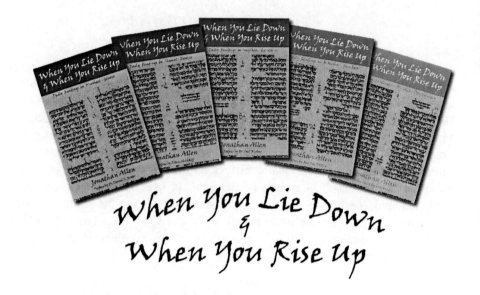

When You Lie Down & When You Rise Up

Daily Readings Following The Weekly Torah Portions

Rabbi Jonathan Allen

www.elishevapublishing.co.uk

CPSIA information can be obtained at www.ICGtesting.com
Printed in the USA
LVOW05s1851150814

399354LV00027B/1017/P